Learning Technology and the Hearing Impaired

258

Learning Technology and the Hearing Impaired

Frank B. Withrow, Ph.D., Editor

What did the clown do?

Volta Review

Vol. 83, No. 5, September 1981, ISSN 0042-8639

The Volta Review is published seven times yearly in January, February-March, April, May, September, October-November, and December. Second-class postage paid at Washington, DC.Copyright © 1981 by the Alexander Graham Bell Association for the Deaf, Inc. Address changes should be sent to the subscription department at the above address and should be received six weeks prior to change.

Table of Contents

Introduction

IIIIIIIIIIIIIIIIIIIIIIIIIIIIIIIIIIIIIIIIIIIIIIIIIIIIIIIIIIIIIIIIIIIIIIIIIIIIIIIIIIIIIIIIIIIIIIIIIIIIIIIIIIIIIII

I n its landmark report in 1970, the Presidential Commission on Instructional Technology concluded that "a society hurtling into the age of computers and satellites can no longer be held back by an educational system which is limping along at the blackboard-and-textbook state of communication."

This monograph brings together a number of professionals who have been working towards a better application of technology to learning for hearing-impaired children. You will find throughout the articles an adherence to "life-long learning." Perhaps no other group in our society requires so much in the way of a life of learning than the hearing impaired. Submerged in a sea of auditory information, the individual with a hearing impairment must constantly struggle upstream to stay even. Technology offers an escape from this imposed isolation and transposes some audio systems into visual messages. The widespread adaptation of captions to television opens up new sources of information for both young and old in the home and in the classroom.

Promises of newer and more exotic technology which can turn print into speech and speech into print will open new opportunities for the hearing impaired to communicate with normally hearing people through telecommunications. Computers in the classroom and in the home will provide the very young hearing-impaired child wider and earlier language experiences. Castle discusses methods for teaching hearing-impaired individuals the use of telecommunications devices for the deaf and other telephone systems. Stuckless describes the use of print in classroom environments and the potential it has for a broader development of language.

Richardson's discussion of the interaction of hearing-impaired children in Hawaii, Illinois, and Washington, D.C., demonstrates the broad implications of computer networks for new means of communication among the hearing impaired. Withrow's detailed language lessons using computer graphics shows how new technologies can be designed to interact with the learner to build solid foundations for language development. The computer terminal knows no discrimination against the hearing impaired. The keyboard offers equal access to all users.

As new technologies come into our home and classrooms teachers must be trained to accept and use these resources. With cutbacks in enrollment and reductions in funds it is essential that teachers learn how to use new technologies effectively. In his history of the use of technology in the education of the hearing impaired, Stepp has emphasized the importance of good teacher training. Such training will be even more important in the immediate future since it is likely that many schools and programs for the hearing impaired will find that they are operating with a smaller staff composed of teachers who are older and more stable. While experienced teachers are positive factors in the education of hearing-impaired children, they can also be a barrier to new technologies. In the past, at least 10% to 15% of the teaching staff entered the field annually. This assured us of an influx of new blood and new ideas from teacher training institutions. With a stable teaching force, this source of new ideas is no longer available.

Both the schools and the training institutions require reorientation towards this new reality of the educational world. Trainers are confronted with a decreasing demand for their products and schools are faced with reduced staff needs. In order to remain viable, programs for staff development must be put into place. This is much more than the normal approach to additional college credits, workshops, and summer schools. It requires an ongoing and continuous planned program of staff development whose goal is increased competence in education of the hearing-impaired child, including the development of competencies in educational technologies. Such an approach will increase the alternatives open to hearing-impaired children and their families and enable more children to realize their potential.

Carl Sagan adequately described our perspective when he said:

Before the invention of writing, human knowledge was restricted to what one person or a small group could remember. . . . After the invention of writing, it was possible to collect, integrate and utilize the accumulated wisdom of all times and all people. . . .

When all is said and done, the invention of writing must be reckoned not only as a brilliant innovation but as a surpassing good for humanity. And assuming that we survive long enough to use their inventions wisely, I believe the same will be said of (those) who are today devising computers and programs at the edge of machine intelligence. The next major structural development in human intelligence is likely to be a partnership between intelligent humans and intelligent machines.

Educational Media and Technology for the Hearing-Impaired Learner: An Historical Overview

1

Robert E. Stepp, Jr.

I nstructional materials have always been part of the teaching/learning process. The resources most frequently used are books, pictures, toys and games, chalkboards, bulletin boards, flash cards, charts, workbooks, and manuals. In the 1930s, motion pictures became an important mode of communication. Other refinements in "technology," such as television, were not available to educational programs until after World War II. The application of these special materials was even further delayed in the education of hearing-impaired children. It was not until 1958 that captioned films for the deaf became a national program (Goldberg, 1980; Stepp, 1980).

"The development and ultimate success of a deaf person hinges, more than all else, on his ability to communicate — to initiate and propagate ideas — and to interpret communications from other persons and from the environment" (Perrin, 1969). To accomplish this objective, it is logical that communication devices and resources of all kinds should be employed extensively in the student's educational program. "General educators have asked, 'What is so special about special education?' A partial answer to this question is that education is primarily a process of communication between the learner and his society. The handicapped child frequently has a break-down in the ability to participate in this process of communication" (Gough, 1968). Without communication an individual cannot assimilate his or her culture. In a society where the spoken word is dominant, it is difficult for hearing-impaired individuals to become fully participating members. Effective receptive and expressive communication is necessary for all members of a society.

The hearing-impaired student's handicap may limit him or her to a sheltered interpretation of the world and thereby restrict learning and social experiences. Educational media and technology can be a new window through which the world may be viewed and shared without barriers. They

Dr. Stepp is Project Director of the Media Development Project for the Hearing Impaired at Teachers College in Lincoln, Nebraska.

provide a simulated learning experience through which the student can step into life in the real world.

Media may also be a vehicle for self-expression. Not only may students react to the materials being used in their learning program, they may use the same or similar materials in their responses to teachers, parents, and peers. Students may express ideas through materials that they have selected, designed, or produced. Thus it is evident educational media and technology can play an increasingly vital role in the education of hearing-impaired students.

Historical Overview

According to Gough (1968), "a special effort to overcome one of the most severe of all communication problems — that of the deaf child — began with the founding of Captioned Films for the Deaf in 1958."

The idea of captioning films for the hearing impaired originated in the late 40s in a doctoral dissertation by Ross Hamilton. This study involved the use of two cameras — one for the movie and one for the captions. As a result of interest in this dissertation topic, Clarence O'Connor and Edmund B. Boatner proposed that similar captioned materials be systematically provided for the deaf (Propp, 1978).

In 1950, the Junior League of Hartford, Connecticut donated a sum of money to establish the first captioned film program in the nation, and Captioned Films for the Deaf, Inc. was organized as a nonprofit corporation. In time, the corporation acquired a library of 30 captioned feature films which were rented to schools for the deaf (Kundert, 1966).

The Library of Congress was asked to consider providing Captioned Films for the Deaf as a service to the hearing impaired in a manner similar to other services provided for the blind (Connor, 1975). As a result, the national office of Captioned Films for the Deaf was made possible by the enactment of Public Law 85-905 in 1958, and the program became operational in October 1959 under the directorship of John A. Gough. Arrangements were negotiated with the major film companies to caption selected entertainment films with exclusive rights to show them to adult deaf clubs and organizations throughout the nation. Research and experimentation was conducted to determine the best method and location for these captions and, as a result, a new technique of printing white letters on a black shadow around each word was perfected (Propp, 1978).

The success of captioning entertainment films led logically to captioning educational films. There are now some 60 libraries in the United States distributing these films to schools for the deaf (Propp, 1978). In 1966, the Educational Media Distribution Center was established in Washington, D.C. to manage the operation of the libraries and to handle an expanded program, funded by P.L. 89-258 in 1965. Filmstrips, slides, transparencies, and other audiovisual materials were added to the extensive selection of films for distribution to schools for the deaf.

Captioned Films services involve more than just the captioning and distribution process. A mechanism for screening and selecting films for captioning has been established; study guides are developed annually for the new films entered into the educational library; workshops are conducted for writing captions; and catalogs are printed and disseminated (Parlato, 1977).

Because of the great demand for films, Congress enlarged the program in 1962, raising the budget ceiling to $1.5 million and adding authority to produce films, provide training in their use with the deaf, and conduct research (Kundert, 1966). Further expansion included the distribution of overhead projectors, filmstrip projectors, screens, and other related audiovisual equipment to schools for the deaf. This program was so effective that in 1967 Congress authorized Captioned Films for the Deaf to extend similar services to all schools for the handicapped. In January 1967, Captioned Films for the Deaf became the Media Services and Captioned Films Branch (Gough, 1968) under the newly established Bureau of Education for the Handicapped (BEH).

Special Education Instructional Materials Network

Parallel to the growth of captioned films and equally significant was the development of a Special Education Instructional Materials Network. In 1964 two Special Education Instructional Materials Centers (SEIMCs), at the University of Wisconsin and the University of Southern California, were funded by the U.S. Office of Education to establish model resource facilities. The success of these two programs resulted in the formation of 14 regional Instructional Materials Centers (Olshin, 1968).

During this same period, Project Hurdle at New Mexico State University conducted an extensive series of in-service workshops in schools for the deaf and was instrumental in stimulating an interest in educational media and technology among teachers (Hester, 1969). In 1964, 8mm color cartridge-load, loop films were designed to teach speechreading on an experimental basis (Stepp, 1965). As a result, Captioned Films supported a collaborative arrangement for the production of a series of 8mm films to teach the first 330 nouns in the basic elementary language of a young hearing-impaired learner.

In 1966, four Regional Media Centers for the Deaf (RMCDs), sponsored by Captioned Films for the Deaf, were founded at the University of Massachusetts, University of Tennessee, New Mexico State University, and the University of Nebraska-Lincoln. These centers conducted media training programs of workshops and institutes for teachers, supervisors, media specialists, administrators, and college professors; produced special instructional materials for the hearing-impaired student; provided media services to programs in designated regions; and sponsored conferences and symposia.

Each RMCD had a unique function in addition to the services already identified. The Northeast Center designed, produced, and distributed transparencies; the Southern Center worked in the area of educational television; the Southwest Center specialized in preparing programmed instructional materials; and the Midwest Center continued its production of 8mm films. This specialization gave added depth to the workshops, institutes, and conferences for professional educators teaching the hearing impaired.

The Midwest Center also had the responsibility for an annual national symposium from 1965 through 1974 and from 1978 to the present. The papers presented at these symposia were published each year in a fall issue of the *American Annals of the Deaf* under the title "Research and Utilization of Educational Media for Teaching the Deaf."

Perhaps the greatest impact of the RMCDs was an activity that never gained much visibility. Participants in in-service training projects developed numerous educational products which were taken home and used with hearing-impaired students. These in-service training functions developed production and utilization skills which led to hundreds and hundreds of items of teacher-produced materials which have enhanced the learning of hearing-impaired children (Propp, 1978).

The Media Services and Captioned Films Branch supported other projects and activities which had further impact on educational media and technology for the hearing impaired. For example, the Programmed Learning Electronic Assembly Program for the Deaf was one of the first major programmed vocational skills learning packages available to train and retrain the deaf in a marketable job skill. Another project was the educational and media technology doctoral program at Syracuse University. Graduates of this program now have leadership roles in this rapidly expanding field. Also, the Career Media Project conducted at the Technical Vocational Institute in St. Paul, Minnesota was responsible for materials which were highly specialized, but expertly designed and produced.

The Instructional Materials Centers and the Regional Media Centers for the Deaf were later merged into one Network composed of 13 regional SEIMCs, four Regional Media Centers for the Deaf, the Instructional Materials Reference Center of the American Printing House for the Blind, the Council for Exceptional Children Information Center on Exceptional Children, the National Center for Educational Media and Materials for the Handicapped, a national coordinating office in Arlington, Virginia, as well as over 300 Associate SEIMCs developed throughout the country through use of local, state, and federal funds (Lance, 1973).

Learning Resources System

In the fall of 1974 the Learning Resources System was established within the Bureau of Education for the Handicapped. This system supplanted the previous network and provided a full range of educational services for all handicapped students, including 1) identification of the handicapped child, 2) diagnosis, 3) program prescription, 4) development of needed instructional materials, and 5) delivery of other appropriate support services to the learner (Norwood, 1974). The two main branches of the network were the Regional Resource Centers (RRCs) and the Area Learning Resource Centers (ALRCs). The nation was divided into 13 regions based on population; each region had a RRC and an ALRC. Both worked with State Education Agencies and while each had its own specific mission — the RRC, to "assure effective appraisal and educational programs for all handicapped children," and the ALRC, to "assure effective instructional materials service to the same population" — they worked closely together in service to the handicapped students of their region (Lance, 1973). The capstone of the ALRC branch of the new system was the continuing National Center for Educational Media and Materials for the Handicapped which maintained a data bank of information about existing and nonexisting-but-needed instructional materials for the handicapped and media-training programs for teachers of the handicapped. The data bank was known as the National Instructional Materials Information System (NIMIS). Also, four Specialized Offices were created. Three of them for the design and production of needed instructional materials, as well as search and location of existing materials — one each for the blind and visually impaired (American Printing House for the Blind), the deaf and hard of hearing learners (University of Nebraska-Lincoln), and the mentally retarded and other handicapping conditions (University of Wisconsin-Madison) — were funded. Information about existing materials was coded for insertion in the NIMIS computer system. Each of the three centers searched and analyzed over 15,000 items. The fourth Specialized Office (University of Indiana) was the "depository for materials and media and distribution services" (Norwood, 1974). Later, the data bank function was transferred to the National Information Center on Educational Materials (NICEM) in Los Angeles at the University of Southern California and was called the National Information Center for Special Education Materials (Baker & Bower, 1980).

In 1974 the Media Services and Captioned Films Branch was renamed the Captioned Films and Telecommunications Branch, still within BEH. This expansion of scope and program led to many significant projects. One widely known project is the Captioned ABC Evening News which was produced under a contract with WGBH-TV in Boston. WGBH-TV also received a grant to caption, experimentally, a series of broadcasts of the

"French Chef" and several telecasts of "Zoom" and incorporated within these activities experimentation and research of various forms of captioning. This type of captioning is referred to as open captioning, meaning that anyone watching the program would see the captions. A contract with the Public Broadcasting Service (PBS) resulted in the development of closed captioning, meaning that anyone wishing to see these captions must have a special decoder attached to his or her television set (see Chapter 3).

Special Centers

Although the Learning Resource Center Network was phased out in 1977, the Captioned Films and Telecommunications Branch did fund two centers to do special assigned tasks. One center was the National Media Materials Center for the Severely Handicapped (NMMCSH) at George Peabody College (now part of Vanderbilt University). Its major accomplishments were 1) the establishment of a retrieval and review system for identifying suitable instructional materials, 2) a program for public information service, 3) a series of learner profiles to be published by the Association for Special Education Technology, and 4) an annual national symposium exploring the instructional needs of the severely handicapped (Symposium, 1978, 1979, 1980).

The other center was the Media Development Project for the Hearing Impaired (MDPHI) at the University of Nebraska-Lincoln which had goals similar to those specified for the NMMCSH. The media search function led to a 3-year study of the reading problems of the hearing impaired and resulted in a series of productions designed to become a syntactically controlled reading program (La Gow, Stoefen, Brunsen, Dam, Kelly, Kingsbury, & Morariu, 1979; Stoefen, 1980). Another phase of the contract resulted in the formation of a national field testing network, a group of more than 100 schools willing to assist the evaluation of the center's new products (Kelly, 1980). A third function was the continuation of an annual symposium similar in scope and purpose to the conferences referred to earlier in this section. The fourth goal was unique — the Project was authorized to explore the potential of the recently developed videodisc as to its application in teaching the hearing impaired. Considerable research has gone into the design and production of a variety of instructional videodiscs which demonstrate applications of this medium in future educational programs for the hearing impaired (Nugent, 1980).

There were several other projects which had a profound impact on the education of the hearing impaired. A significant one was the Children's Television Workshop which produces "Sesame Street." Millions of children watch these programs and those of "The Electric Company" every day (Palmer, 1970). Project LIFE (Language Instruction to Facilitate Education) was also a successful program. Over 300 filmstrips were developed to reduce the language and reading problems of severely hearing-impaired children. These materials are now being distributed by Instructional Industries, Inc., a subsidiary of the General Electric Company (Pfau, 1974). Also, the Elementary and Secondary Education Act of 1965 was one of several laws which provided funds to support special projects for the hearing impaired as well as support to regular programs. This Act had a significant impact on the nonhandicapped and the handicapped student (Propp, 1978).

Where Do We Go From Here?

Meierhenry (1980) in his address on "Learning and Instructional Theory Revisited" at the Nebraska Symposium concluded that:

> 1) A likely major thrust in the years to come is to focus on learners and their characteristics as they impinge upon instructional and media decisions.
> 2) A second major effort is likely to be a much more intensive examination of content to be learned and the selection and design of materials in order to accomplish appropriate objectives.
> 3) Continuing attention is likely to be given to the various environmental factors which facilitate and/or retard effective learning.
> 4) A fourth component likely to be given attention is the development of new technologies along with systematic studies of how these and older technologies contribute to various instructional objectives.

He further commented that "It will not be an era of development of technologies for technologies' sake, but rather an analysis of the unique characteristics of each medium to determine the extent to which it will contribute to certain intellectual tasks expected of the learner." There is no question that educational media and technology will play a greater role in the education of the hearing-impaired learner in the future. We are now beginning to understand the contribution that instructional resources can make.

One significant trend is to select those resources which will promote and require interaction. This refers to a level of learning involvement with media that requires participation in the learning process and also a variety of response modes for feedback (Fox, 1979). The computer is an excellent example of a participatory learning experience. Reinforcement is almost instantaneous and provides a new style of learning sequence and performance.

Another consideration for the future is the interconnection of schools for the hearing impaired by either cable or satellite, resulting in a regional or national network (Bransford, 1978). The feasibility of a network by satellite transmission was demonstrated at the 1979 Nebraska Symposium. A group of educators of the deaf in Washington, D.C. witnessed a demonstration of videodisc technology being presented at a general session of the

Symposium in Nebraska. Two-way video and two-way audio permitted deaf educators to interact with each other without the need of an interpreter (Propp, Nugent, Nugent, & Stone, 1979). One satellite transmission band should be held in reserve for a communication network serving the handicapped in their various education programs, both in school and in the home.

The breakthrough created by technology in developing Line 21 (closed) captioning and videodisc records and players is only the forerunner of the impact that electronics will have on education in general and education of the hearing impaired in particular. Already the electronic games that are being developed and marketed signal a new level of interaction. It is only logical that these devices will have an important role in teaching content, especially language development and mathematics. The "fun aspect" of these games should not be overlooked as a motivation factor in the learning process. Also, with the success of closed captions one now looks forward to the possibility of real-time captioning (McCoy & Shumway, 1979).

A continuing study of the learner characteristics of the hearing-impaired student will not only proceed on its search for more knowledge, but will find new ways, through technology, to study further the brain and its reaction to various forms of stimuli (Kelly, 1978; Stuckless, 1978). A study of cerebral lateralization of the hearing impaired in contrast to the processing of the same information by their normally hearing peers is not only fascinating, but is basic to an understanding of their learning problems. This research is fundamental and essential.

Although an attempt has not been made here to describe historically the development of educational media and technology within the instructional programs at Gallaudet College and the National Technical Institute for the Deaf, there is no question at this writing that these schools play a leadership role in the utilization and production of these resources. Their facilities are designed to encourage use of these materials. The instructional faculties are familiar with these teaching/learning resources and support staffs have the skills to design, develop, and produce a wide variety of materials.

Withrow (1979) stated "new methods of transmission and tele-communications are evolving, new insights into the learning process itself are being explored. Most of all, the new technology truly allows the learner to control and experiment with learning materials." These changes are occurring in schools for the hearing impaired as well as in schools for the normally hearing student. The Captioned Films and Telecommunications Branch has been instrumental in sponsoring these developments at the national level by supporting and promoting the utilization of educational media and technology in programs for the hearing impaired. The major breakthroughs in technology for the hearing impaired have been made possible by this government agency. Advances in technology and future utilization of educational media in instructional programs for the hearing impaired will continue to require cooperation and support at all levels of government. Basic research, media demonstrations, material productions, and professional training are all forms of partnerships. The beneficiaries are the millions of hearing-impaired persons in the United States who depend on educational programs for their improvement in communication skills and development of general knowledge.

REFERENCES

BAKER, D.B., & BOWER, K.B. Update on activities and services of the national information center for special education materials. *Journal of Special Education Technology,* 1980, *3*(3), 11-13.

BRANSFORD, L. Communication satellites: Applications for the hearing impaired. *American Annals of the Deaf,* 1978, *123*(6), 672-678.

CONNOR, L.E. Personal communication, May 27, 1975.

FOX, R. Toward the future in educational systems. *American Annals of the deaf,* 1979, *124*(5), 521-529.

GOLDBERG, L.M. Creative use of media in schools and programs for the hearing impaired. *The Volta Review,* 1980, *82*(6), 440-446.

GOUGH, J.A. Educational media and the handicapped child. *Exceptional Children,* 1968, *34*(7), 561-564.

HESTER, M.S. Southwest regional media center for the deaf. *American Annals of the Deaf,* 1969, *114*(5), 845-846.

KELLY, R.R. Hemispheric specialization of deaf children: Are there any implications for instruction. *American Annals of the Deaf,* 1978, *123*(6), 637-645.

KELLY, R.R. The evaluation program and nationwide field test effort of the Media Development Project for the Hearing Impaired. *American Annals of the Deaf,* 1980, *125*(6), 798-801.

KUNDERT, J.J. *The captioned films for the deaf program.* Washington, DC: U.S. Department of Health, Education, and Welfare, Bureau of Educational Research and Development, 1966.

LA GOW, R., STOEFEN, J., BRUNSEN, J., DAM, L., KELLY, K., KINGSBURY, M., & MORARIU, J. Design and development of a basic reading program for the hearing impaired. *American Annals of the Deaf,* 1979, *124*(5), 635-651.

LANCE, W.D. *Instructional media and the handicapped.* Stanford: ERIC Clearinghouse on Media and Technology, 1973.

McCOY, E., & SHUMWAY, R. Real-time captioning — Promise for the future. *American Annals for the Deaf,* 1979, *124*(5), 681-690.

MEIERHENRY, W.C. Learning and instructional theory revisited. *American Annals of the Deaf,* 1980, *125*(6), 626-631.

NORWOOD, M.J. Future trends. *American Annals of the Deaf,* 1974, *119*(5), 619-623.

NUGENT, G. The videodisc: A tool in teaching the handicapped. *Journal of Special Education Technology,* 1980, *3*(3), 68-70.

OLSHIN, G.J. Special Education Instructional Materials Center program. *Exceptional Children,* 1968, *34*(7), 515-522.

PALMER, E.L. Television's neglected strengths. *American Annals of the Deaf,* 1970, *115*(6), 601-604.

PARLATO, S. Those other captioned films . . . captioned educational films. *American Annals of the Deaf,* 1977, *122*(1), 33-37.

PERRIN, D.G. The role of media in individualized instruction for teaching the deaf. *American Annals of the Deaf,* 1969, *114*(5), 912-919.

PFAU, G.S. Project LIFE a decade later: Some reflections and projections. *American Annals of the Deaf,* 1974, *119*(5), 549-553.

PROPP, G. An overview of progress in utilization of educational technology for educating the hearing impaired. *American Annals of the Deaf,* 1978, *123*(6), 646-652.

PROPP, G., NUGENT, G., NUGENT, R., & STONE, C. Satellite demonstration: The videodisc technology. *American Annals of the Deaf,* 179, *124*(5), 652-655.

STEPP, R.E., Jr. Demonstration of learning laboratory established to facilitate lipreading practice. *American Annals of the Deaf,* 1965, *110*(5), 588-590.

STEPP, R.E., Jr. Utilization of educational media: Introduction. *American Annals of the Deaf,* 1980, *125*(6), 623-625.

STOEFEN, J. Focus on reading: Project update. *American Annals of the Deaf,* 1980, *125*(6), 751-764.

STUCKLESS, R.E. Technology and the visual processing of verbal information by deaf people. *American Annals of the Deaf,* 1978, *123*(6), 630-636.

Symposium, 1978. First annual symposium of the National Media Materials Center for Severely Handicapped Persons: Creating a synergy between consumer and producer: Separating the PRO$ from the CON$. *Journal of Special Education Technology,* 1978, *1*(2).

Symposium, 1979. Second annual symposium of the National Media Materials Center for Severely Handicapped Persons. *Journal of Special Education Technology,* 1979, *2*(4).

Symposium, 1980. Third annual symposium report on media materials for the severely handicapped: The next decade. *Journal of Special Education Technology,* 1980, *3*(3).

WITHROW, F.B. *Educational technology for the learner.* Conference on Interactive Videodisc and Media Storage Technology in Education and Training, Society for Applied Learning Technology, February 1979.

Telecommunication and the Hearing Impaired

2

IIIIIIIIIIIIIIIIIIIIIIIIIIIIIIIIIIIIIIIIIIIIIIIIIIIIIIIIIIIIIIIIIIIIIIIIIIIIIIIIIIIIIIIIIIIIIIIIIIIIIIIIII

Diane L. Castle

F or speech- or hearing-impaired people, telephone communication is a challenge and a frustration. They need special guidance and equipment in order to overcome the problems related to communication at a distance. Until recently, telephone communication by the severely or profoundly hearing-impaired population received very little emphasis (Castle, 1977, 1978a; McLeod & Guenther, 1977; Stoffels, 1980).

As part of their communication training, many severely or profoundly hearing-impaired students at the National Technical Institute for the Deaf in Rochester, New York are taught various techniques to improve their telephone communication skills. A special Telecommunication Lab (Johnson, 1976) and two courses were designed for this purpose. Both courses include general consumer information about the telephone system, emergency phone calls, renting or buying a telephone, saving money on long distance phone calls, etc. Students are enrolled in these courses based on their communication abilities (Castle, 1978b). One course curriculum, *Telephone Training for the Deaf* (Castle, 1980), teaches students use of the standard telephone and communication strategies to overcome problems in speaking with or listening to strangers. The other curriculum, *Telecommunication Training for the Deaf* (Castle, 1981), focuses on use of telephone coding systems with family or friends and telecommunication devices for the deaf.

This article will review some of the information covered in these curricula, as well as other areas of interest. Consumer awareness tips are included also.

Hearing Aids and Telephone Amplifiers

Telecoils. Hearing-impaired people who use the standard telephone usually depend on a hearing aid and/or amplified telephone handset. Many hearing aids have a special "T" (telecoil) setting that improves telephone communication. The small magnetic telecoil in the hearing aid is designed

Dr. Castle is an associate professor at the National Technical Institute for the Deaf in Rochester, New York.

to work in conjunction with the magnetic leakage from telephone receivers. When the hearing aid is set on "T" the magnetic field around the telephone receiver (handset) is picked up by the telecoil in the hearing aid. The magnetic signal is changed into sound by the hearing aid. When using the "T" setting, sound is not picked up by the hearing aid microphone ("M" setting).

Hearing-impaired persons tend to prefer to use the "T" setting because it is easier to concentrate on the telephone conversation; when compared with the magnetic signal picked up by the hearing aid, other sounds in the room are significantly reduced in loudness. In addition, using the "T" setting frequently eliminates the problem of hearing aid feedback caused by a loose earmold. Feedback occurs more often when using a hearing aid on the "M" setting. A potential disadvantage with the "T" setting is that hearing-impaired persons cannot hear their voices through the hearing aid, but must monitor their speech production by listening to their voices coming through the telephone receiver. In this situation, their speech may sound different than speech monitored through the "M" setting.

Built-in Amplifier. Contrary to popular belief, the amplified handset offers substantial assistance to the severely and profoundly hearing-impaired person using a hearing aid. The additional gain supplied by the amplified handset makes it easier to hear the other person without straining to listen, especially when calling long distance, when a hearing aid battery is weak, or when talking with someone who has a soft voice. Any hearing aid setting can be used with an amplifier.

The amplified handset should give the hearing-impaired person both greater acoustic gain and greater magnetic leakage. The acoustic gain is desirable for the individual who uses the amplified handset without a hearing aid or in conjunction with a hearing aid set on "M." The increased magnetic leakage is only necessary when the hearing aid is used on the "T" setting. Some amplified handsets may contain a receiver that does not increase the magnetic leakage although there is increased acoustic gain. It is important for the consumer to be aware of this possibility and be able to explain the problem in order to effect a solution.

The built-in amplifier can be purchased or rented from the telephone company. If it is working properly, the intensity of speech or sound can be increased by 25dB to 30dB when adjusting the volume dial on the handset (Hammer, 1964). When the dial is returned to zero, the telephone handset works without amplification and can be used by any normally hearing person.

The Portable Amplifier. Several companies manufacture a small, battery-operated, portable amplifier that slips over the telephone handset, but it is useful only on telephones with sufficient magnetic leakage. The built-in amplifier has more acoustic gain than the portable one. A hearing-impaired person should try both kinds of amplifiers to determine which one is more satisfactory. The portable amplifier can be purchased from a local hearing aid dealer or an electronic or stereo shop.

The Adapter. On some telephones (e.g., public pay phones, Slimline, Trimline, or designer models), there is insufficient magnetic leakage to enable the hearing-impaired person to hear when using the "T" setting (Smith, 1974). A portable battery-operated adapter was designed to strengthen the magnetic field to permit use of the "T" setting. However, many severely and profoundly hearing-impaired persons find it does not provide sufficient loudness and clarity on incompatible telephones (Organization for the Use of the Telephone, 1980).

Telecommunication Devices for the Deaf

Before telecommunication devices for the deaf (TDDs) were available, a hearing-impaired person with limited speaking or listening skills had to rely on the assistance of another person to make a telephone call. Independent telephone communication between two hearing-impaired people with limited auditory-oral communication skills was not possible until 1964, when Robert Weitbrecht designed a coupler (acoustic modem) that made it possible to transmit and receive typed information from one location to another through standard telephone lines. With the use of reconditioned surplus teletype equipment and the acoustic coupler, these hearing-impaired citizens had an opportunity to use the telephone without relying on their speaking or listening skills.

To communicate by teletypewriter, one person dials the number of another person having compatible equipment, places the telephone receiver in a special coupler, and waits for the other person to answer the telephone. The person answering places his or her receiver in a similar coupler and begins typing. Simultaneously, the same words are printed out by the other teletypewriter. A hearing-impaired person using this kind of equipment can have local and long distance telephone communication with any other person having a TDD.

In the 1970s, new, rather than reconditioned, teletypewriters became available to hearing-impaired people. At present, there are at least 10 to 15 different manufacturers, some with two or three different models for sale (Stoffels, 1980). Special features may vary with different models. Possible features include portability; a paper printout of the conversation; a display area for seeing the typed conversation; a memory for storing messages; red, blue, or green letters; direct connection to the telephone line; and rental from the telephone company.

The selection of a TDD is very personal and depends on the particular needs of the individual and the environment in which the TDD will be used. For example, an individual with visual problems may select a TDD with large, clear print. A person with limited space in the home or office may select a small portable TDD. On the other hand, a person working in a library environment may select a TDD that is very quiet. Therefore, interested persons should try the various types of equipment commercially available before deciding which one to purchase.

Growing publicity regarding TDDs has helped to encourage their installation in various emergency facilities, churches, libraries, government offices, community service organizations, etc. A number of businesses which employ deaf persons have purchased TDDs to allow them to contact their homes during the work day. Travel facilities such as airlines, airports, hotels, travel agencies, and Amtrak have installed TDDs. In addition, many travel facilities, businesses, and government offices have installed toll-free TDD numbers. In June 1980, the Bell Telephone System installed a special nationwide toll-free TDD number that allows TDD users to get assistance from a telephone operator.

There are two different kinds of electronic codes used by teleprinters: Baudot and ASCII. The acoustic coupler, used by the hearing impaired for telephone communication, was designed to work with the Baudot code because that kind of surplus equipment code was easily obtained and inexpensive. Computer terminals use ASCII, but they were very expensive at that time.

In order to be compatible with each other, TDDs must use 1) the 5-bit Baudot code, 2) audio-tone frequencies of 1400 and 1800 Hz, and 3) an audio-tone transmission rate at 45.5 bits per second. These machines operate at speeds of up to 60 words per minute and are not directly compatible with computer terminals.

At present, the Baudot code is used by fewer and fewer commercial facilities. It appears to be limited to use by the TDD network, Radio ham operators, and the UPI news service (Strassler, 1980).

Today, personal home computers, large computers used by commercial companies, telephone companies, and communications carriers are using ASCII. ASCII machines type at a much faster speed and have greater flexibility because they can be used both as computer terminals and as communication devices. It seems there is increasing interest on the part of TDD manufacturers to include an ASCII option in addition to the Baudot code.

Electronic Handwriters

For certain hearing-impaired populations, a communication device that does not require typing skills may be useful. There has been some interest in electronic writing equipment which can use telephone or direct wire connections to send and/or receive handwritten messages across any distance. This type of equipment is often used in hospitals, industry, and business to speed communications. In addition, technical information can be sketched or diagrammed during the conversation. This type of device may have application in special types of situations that face the hearing impaired at home or work.*

Telephone Devices for the Deaf-Blind

Several devices have been specifically designed to make telephone communication possible for the deaf-blind. At least two pieces of equipment are commercially available at this time: the Code-Com and the Braille-TTY. Other devices are under development at the Helen Keller National Center for Deaf-Blind Youth and Adults (Kruger & Rosenfeld, 1976).

The Code-Com is a nonportable attachment to the telephone that converts sound signals into visual or tactile signals. Using a yes-no code or Morse code to receive information, the deaf person can see or feel that pattern while a deaf-blind person can feel the incoming message. To send a message, the deaf or deaf-blind person can speak or use Morse code. The Code-Com is available through the Bell Telephone Company.

A Braille-Teletypewriter allows a deaf-blind person to communicate with other standard TDDs by converting the incoming typed conversation into Braille while the outgoing message is sent in standard typed form. The deaf-blind person reads the telephone conversation by moving his or her fingertips across the raised dots on the paper.

Telephone Coding Systems

Another approach to independent use of the telephone is with a code system. A code uses special words, numbers, sounds, or letters for communication. The hearing-impaired person may be able to detect the code through the use of a hearing aid and/or an amplified handset. For the hearing-impaired person who cannot detect sound through audition, a visual code indicator can be purchased.** Speech codes or nonspeech codes can be used to give information on the telephone.

Speech Codes. The yes-no code is optimal when the conversation has a specific topic of discussion and is relatively brief. It is not like a real conversation. Typically, the hearing-impaired person initiates the call, controls the conversation, and has the responsibility for giving information and asking questions. The normally hearing person responds with a pre-

---

*There are several companies including Victor Graphics Systems, Inc., Telautograph Corp., and Talos Systems, Inc. that distribute the Electrowriter, Telepen, and Telenote, respectively.

**S.G. Barnes and Associates, 31316 Via Colinas, Suite 105, Westlake Village, CA 91361

arranged code. A frequently used code between hearing and hearing-impaired persons consists of a basic one-, two-, or three-beat rhythm pattern. This pattern can serve as the code for "no," "yes-yes/o-k," or "please repeat," respectively. For some hearing-impaired persons, a voice response may be too soft and difficult to hear, and it may be easier to hear the rhythm pattern when tapping on or blowing air into the telephone mouthpiece.

A code system can be created, modified, or expanded for the hearing-impaired person who discriminates selected words, numbers, letters, or sentences (McLeod & Guenther, 1977). In that situation, the communication becomes more balanced, allowing the normally hearing person to initiate conversation also. The 10-code used by CB operators is an example of how numbers can be used in a code instead of words and sentences.

Nonspeech Codes. Code systems which do not require intelligible speech, such as the use of Morse code or special code arrangements with the Touch-Tone telephone, can be used to send and receive information over the telephone (Flanagan, 1968; Levitt & Nelson, 1970; Smith, 1965). Once the code is learned, both people can participate equally in the conversation. Anyone can develop their own code system; however, these codes require training and practice before the communication is smooth and efficient. It is important to explain the code and to practice using the code system with the people that will be called. Using a code system often requires more time, patience, and perseverance than other communication forms.

Speech Indicator. If the hearing-impaired person cannot hear the other person's code, a speech indicator can show the rhythm pattern for codes. It also shows when the dial tone, busy signal, and ringing sounds occur. This equipment is portable, relatively inexpensive, and connects to the telephone with a small rubber suction cup.

Radio Paging Equipment

As with electronic handwriters, radio pagers are used by the normally hearing population and also have been useful to hearing-impaired persons. For example, radio pagers that transmit voice or a tone can also transmit a vibrotactile signal. This kind of paging equipment would make it possible to contact a profoundly hearing-impaired child or adult at a distance from, but within the radius of, the equipment. The vibrating signal can be used as a coded telephone call to alert a hearing-impaired person to telephone for more information, to go to a prearranged location, or to perform a certain activity.

A hearing-impaired person who is able to understand some words and sentences through hearing may be able to understand a limited verbal message over the radio pager. In addition, some hearing-impaired people may be able to detect the sound of the low pitched tone from a standard pager when wearing a hearing aid.

Consumer Awareness Tips

The following information is designed to guide the reader with regard to some of the equipment discussed; that is, certain advantages and disadvantages; areas of controversy; points to consider prior to purchase; where to purchase; general consumer information; and names of certain consumer organizations.

The Telecoil. The "T" setting in hearing aids is not standardized. Severely or profoundly hearing-impaired persons who use the "T" setting on the hearing aid may experience insufficient gain as compared with the "M" setting. Only a few models from different hearing aid manufacturers will provide comparable gain regardless of the setting. In addition, some people may find that the location of the telecoil inside the hearing aid case is not positioned for best telephone use. Before buying a hearing aid, one should be sure to evaluate both the "M" and "T" settings. Dialing a standard tape-recorded message is a good way to compare the relative loudness of each setting.

Amplifiers. Built-in amplifiers may vary in performance. Some amplifiers are stronger than others. After a period of use, a built-in amplifier may lose some of its original loudness.

The portable amplifier may be bulky or uncomfortable for some people to use in comparison with the built-in amplifier. However, purchasing a portable amplifier offers a long-term savings over the rental of a built-in amplifier. Because large scale distributors such as Radio Shack buy in large quantities, their portable amplifiers cost considerably less than those typically sold by hearing aid dealers. Telecoil users should remember that the portable amplifier will not work with all telephones. Its use will be limited to those telephones having a strong magnetic leakage. Many telephones installed in residences, businesses, and hospitals are not compatible with the "T" setting because of weak magnetic leakage.

The Adapter. As discussed earlier, this device is not a solution to the problem of incompatibility between hearing aids and telephones. However, the Bell System is continuing to experiment with various solutions. The Organization for the Use of the Telephone, Inc. (OUT)* founded in 1973, has been responsible for promoting increased awareness of problems relating to telephone and hearing aid compatibility. Recently, OUT urged the Architectural and Transportation Barriers Compliance Board to require that all telephones in public buildings be compatible with telecoil settings and that TDDs be provided. In 1977, the Consumers Organization for the

---

*Organization for the Use of the Telephone, Inc., P.O. Box 175, Owings Mills, MD 21117

Hearing Impaired (COHI)* was formed to organize the hearing-impaired population on a variety of consumer issues.

Items Relating to TDDs.   Before buying a TDD, the consumer should be sure to try using the various types of equipment currently available and decide which features are important. For example: Is paper needed? Is portability wanted? The consumer should compare the feel of each keyboard, the print size, color, readability, and consider how long the company has been manufacturing TDDs. He or she should also check on availability of local on-site repair, approximately how long it will take to obtain service, and how much service will cost. It is also important to ask friends about their experiences with different TDDs. In general, the non-portable TDDs have greater dependability and less need for repair. Some companies offer discounts when TDDs are purchased in quantity. At the minimum, the nonportable TDD will have a lifespan of 10 to 20 years while a portable TDD should function for 5 to 10 years.

TDD numbers for police, fire, ambulance, and other emergencies are seldom published in the telephone directory. Most cities have a deaf club or telecommunication association that collects and publishes, for members, a listing of TDD emergency and general information numbers. In the future, several telephone companies indicate they plan to publish these important TDD numbers in the local telephone directories. Telecommunications for the Deaf, Inc. (TDI)** publishes TDD numbers annually in the *International Telephone Directory of the Deaf.*

In order to have your name and TDD number listed in the Directory, you must become a member. They list toll-free TDD numbers of businesses that have installed TDDs, authorized sales representatives for different TDDs in each state, and other useful information. TDI is an important resource for information relating to TDDs.

Until recently, it was not possible for hearing-impaired people to obtain operator services when using TDDs. In June 1980, the Bell Telephone system established a toll free TDD number: 1-800-855-1155. A telephone operator, using a TDD, is available every day of the week at all hours, offering local and long distance services to hearing-impaired persons.

Because it takes more time to communicate by typing than by voice, many states have reduced long distance *intra*state rates for TDD users. Several telephone companies rent, or plan to rent, TDDs which offers the consumer the advantage of local repair service rather than sending the TDD to another part of the country. Contact your telephone company to determine which special services or discounts they offer.

The ASCII code is available in several TDDs. However, it appears that the primary advantage for the hearing-impaired consumer would be

---

*Consumers Organization for the Hearing Impaired, Inc., P.O. Box 2538, Laurel, MD 20811

**Telecommunications for the Deaf, Inc., 814 Thayer Ave., Silver Spring, MD 20910

related to saving money on toll or long distance calls since the message is transmitted very quickly when both people use ASCII. Applied Communications Corporation has developed the Phonetype 80 which, when attached to an ASCII terminal, will work with Baudot or ASCII codes. This equipment makes it possible for ASCII terminals to communicate with the TDD network. In the future, persons using an ASCII terminal would be able to contact banks, airline ticket agencies, department stores, news services, weather reports, library services, hospitals, etc. At present, those kinds of services are not yet available and may not be for 4 to 5 years. Experimental projects involving ASCII terminals in selected communities with deaf persons are ongoing (Cerf, 1978).

Training in Telephone Usage

Many hearing-impaired people who could speak and/or listen over the telephone lack experience and confidence in their ability to understand or be understood. Those with more limited communication skills are not familiar with the telephone system, the variety of TDDs, and telephone coding systems. The National Technical Institute for the Deaf, through its telephone training programs, has taught severely and profoundly hearing-impaired students various ways to manage telephone communication. These techniques should become more widespread. Hearing-impaired adults may benefit from more opportunities for continuing education relating to use of the telephone and telephone coding systems. Hearing-impaired youngsters of school age could be encouraged to learn some of these various methods of telephone communication. Because of its experience in this unique training area, NTID has been a resource for providing information to the hearing-impaired adult, to parents and friends of the hearing impaired, to educators of the hearing impaired, audiologists, speech pathologists, vocational rehabilitation counselors, etc.

ACKNOWLEDGMENT

The materials herein were produced in the course of an agreement between the Rochester Institute of Technology and the U.S. Department of Education.

REFERENCES

CASTLE, D.L. Telephone training for the deaf. *The Volta Review,* 1977, *79*(6), 373-378.
CASTLE, D.L. Telephone communication for the hearing impaired: Methods and equipment. *Journal of the Academy of Rehabilitative Audiology,* 1978, *11,* 91-104. (a)
CASTLE, D.L. Letter to the editor. *The Volta Review,* 1978, *80*(2), 119-120. (b)
CASTLE, D.L. *Telephone training for the deaf.* Rochester, NY: National Technical Institute for the Deaf, 1980.
CASTLE, D.L. *Telecommunication training for the deaf.* Rochester, NY: National Technical Institute for the Deaf, 1981.

CERF, V. The electronic mailbox: A new communication tool for the hearing impaired. *American Annals of the Deaf,* 1978, *123,* 768-772.

FLANAGAN, J.L. New approaches in telephone use by the deaf. In H.G. Kopp, (Ed.) *Accent on unity – Horizons on deafness, Proceedings of National Forum 1, Council of Organizations Serving the Deaf,* Washington, D.C., 1968.

HAMMER, K.E. Handsets with transistor amplifiers. *Bell Laboratories Record.* May 1964, 159-164.

JOHNSON, D.D. Laboratory design for instruction in telecommunication for the deaf. In D.D. Johnson & W.E. Castle (Eds.), *Infoseries 2.* Rochester, NY: National Technical Institute for the Deaf, 1976.

KRUGER, F.M., & ROSENFELD, J. *The role of technology in deaf-blind communication.* Paper presented at Conference on Systems and Devices for the Disabled, Boston, 1976.

LEVITT, H., & NELSON, J.R. Experimental communication aids for the deaf. *IEEE Transactions on Audio and Electroacoustics,* 1970, *18,* 2-6.

MCLEOD, R., JR., & GUENTHER, M. Use of an ordinary telephone by an oral deaf person: A case history. *The Volta Review,* 1977, *79*(7), 435-442.

Organization for the Use of the Telephone, Inc. Out meets with AT&T. *The Out-Line,* October 23, 1980.

SMITH, G.M. What hath God wrought? *The Volta Review,* 1965, *67*(7), 505-507.

SMITH, G.M. The telephone adapter and other telephone aids for the hard of hearing. *The Volta Review,* 1974, *76*(8), 474-484.

STOFFELS, B. Telecommunications devices for the deaf. *Telephone Engineer and Management,* October 1, 1980, pp. 69-73.

STRASSLER, B. The ASCII-Baudot dilemma. *The Silent News,* March 1980, p. 18.

Closed-Captioned Television and the Hearing Impaired 3

||||||||||||||||||||||||||||||||||||||||||||||||||||||||||||||||||||||||||||||||||||||||||||||||||||||||||||

Doris C. Caldwell

Citizens of all ages whose hearing is impaired can now watch many of the same television programs at the same time and with the same understanding as the general population. Although hearing-impaired consumers have owned TV sets and watched programs for years, the screen has presented little more than a series of animated pictures. Now, closed captions transform the same television screen into a primary source of information and entertainment which has long been available to the normally hearing world.

Closed captioning is a process in which the dialogue portion of a television program is translated into captions (subtitles), converted to electronic codes, and inserted in the regular broadcast television signal in a portion of the picture which is normally not seen. In order to see the captions, viewers must have televisions equipped with special decoding devices available as adapters or integrated receivers. (In contrast, "open" captions are broadcast as part of the program and appear on all television sets.)

To close caption a television program, the producer furnishes a video-tape of the program to a National Captioning Institute captioning facility prior to the broadcast date. There, caption editors transform the spoken dialogue into captions which are recorded on a magnetic disc. The disc is sent to the television broadcaster where the caption data is inserted onto Line 21 of the TV picture. (A television picture is actually made up of a number of beamed lines, some of which are blank. Line 21 is normally a blank line.) The broadcaster then transmits the caption data along with the regular picture and sound portions of the program.

History of Closed Captioning

The concept of inserting hidden information in the broadcast signal is almost as old as television itself. Since the mid-1950s, program broadcasts have often contained engineering test signals which never appear on the

Ms. Caldwell is Special Assistant to the President of the National Captioning Institute in Falls Church, Virginia.

television screen. By the late 60s, continued advances in electronic circuit technology made it possible for more widespread and sophisticated use to be made of these hidden signals.

In December 1971, the National Bureau of Standards and the ABC Television Network demonstrated a system which would allow captions to be seen only on television sets equipped with special decoding devices. By June 1972, a subcommittee established by the National Association of Broadcasters reported that such a system was technically feasible but required further research and development before it could be implemented. Subsequent discussions between the Public Broadcasting Service (PBS) and the U.S. Bureau of Education for the Handicapped (BEH) led to the first contract in February 1973 for development of the closed-captioning technology. The Federal Communications Commission authorized temporary use of Line 21, and the first experimental closed-captioned broadcasts aired.

By the end of 1974, important information had been gained through analyses of data collected from over 1,400 test-audience questionnaires: 1) basic guidelines related to the captions themselves (e.g., presentation rates, editing procedures, size of font, background shading, and other factors related to visibility and readability); 2) 90% of the hearing-impaired respondents said the captions made the programs far more understandable; 3) 96% wanted to buy decoders for home use although no cost figure had been mentioned; and 4) PBS engineers had thoroughly evaluated test transmissions and were ready to proceed with development of the closed-captioning system.

In December 1976, the Federal Communications Commission formally reserved Line 21 for the transmission of closed captions and thus cleared the way for extending the benefits of television to hearing-impaired Americans for the first time. PBS accelerated its completion of the technical and operational aspects. Meanwhile, negotiations began on other fronts to secure network support for closed captioning and to ensure mass production sales of low-cost decoding units for home use.

In March 1979, Health, Education, and Welfare Secretary Joseph Califano announced: the National Captioning Institute (NCI), a nonprofit corporation, had been established to provide and promote the unique closed-captioning service; ABC, NBC, and PBS had agreed to participate in the service; and home-use decoding equipment (TeleCaption) would be marketed by Sears, Roebuck and Co.

Present Status of Closed Captioning

The closed-captioning service offered by the National Captioning Institute (NCI) has experienced steady growth during its first year of operation — national programming up from 16 to at least 25 hours per week and expanding from prime time into daytime programs; more than 100 major advertisers (as of May 1981) committed to having their commercials and specials captioned; syndicators, independent producers, and other broadcasters participating in increasing numbers; and closed-captioned videotapes for classroom instruction and home entertainment beginning to appear in the marketplace.

Outpourings of delight and gratitude from hearing-impaired viewers continue to mount. This enthusiastic response has caught the attention of major service organizations across the United States who have implemented special projects to increase public awareness and aid those who need and want the service but cannot afford to buy it. TeleCaption equipment is available in two versions: a portable adapter unit which can be easily attached to any television set and a 19" color television with built-in decoding circuitry.

The most dramatic technical development during NCI's first operational year was the "live" captioning of sports spectaculars and important public events. Scoreboard information was transmitted from the stadium to owners of decoding devices during the Sugar Bowl and Super Bowl games in January 1981. The 1981 Presidential Inaugural ceremony and subsequent addresses to the nation by President Reagan have also been successfully closed captioned.

The term "live" is used in this instance to refer to captions which are prepared from advance copies of speeches and stored in computer memory to be later replayed in pace with a speaker's actual delivery. Live captioning is a major milestone in the long developmental history of the Line 21 system, marking the final step toward "real-time" (simultaneous) captioning of national newscasts, sports commentary, and public affairs events as they occur.

Educational and Psychosocial Impact

Parents and educators recognize that well-written captions directly attack communications problems faced by hearing-impaired learners — reading, writing, vocabulary building, semantic understanding, grammar, and all elements of overall linguistic competence. Teachers and media specialists in schools for the hearing impaired across the country report their young students eagerly watch captioned TV shows (recorded on videotape cassettes) over and over again to absorb the words on the screen. They are motivated to read by the pleasant environment of television. Captioned TV programs enliven the classroom environment and extend effective learning into after-school hours. Improved reading and comprehension skills inevitably lead to improved achievement in all academic disciplines.

Adult deaf persons, too, have commented on their noted increases in vocabulary. Since everyone depends upon reading to provide or supplement verbal information, it is logical to assume that skill in reading captions may be enhanced by the intensity of hearing-impaired peoples' desire to understand the content of a television series which has long titillated their interest and curiosity on the strength of its appeal to the visual sense alone. Indeed, well-constructed captions can be considered a form of continuing education for hearing-impaired persons of all ages.

There is mounting evidence that closed captioning is far more than a technological breakthrough; it is a sociological and psychological triumph as well. Hearing-impaired people of all ages are now able to communicate more freely with their normally hearing families and peers as they share current information and entertainment. This new access to the pervasive world of TV appears to be exerting a powerful influence on the lives of hearing-impaired viewers and breaking down communications barriers which historically have inhibited their efforts to mingle fully in society's mainstream.

Future Plans and International Outreach

While the basic technology of the Line 21 system is sound and firmly entrenched, closed captioning of popular TV programs is merely a stepping stone to other innovative services to hearing-impaired audiences and others. Areas under development include: 1) closed captions on film as well as videotape; 2) second-language captioning; 3) real-time captioning of newscasts, sports, and other events; 4) a full-screen "printed radio" tentatively called Infodata; and 5) compatibility with television broadcasting formats and equipment, such as teletext systems, used in other countries. Progress on all these fronts is unfolding rapidly.

The success of closed captioning and the enthusiastic acclaim from hearing-impaired Americans have not gone unnoticed in other countries. Canadian broadcasters have unanimously adopted the Line 21 system, and closed captions went on the air in that country in January 1981. Keen expressions of interest from around the world have prompted NCI to propose an international exchange of closed-captioned programs and technical information with other English-speaking nations.

Conclusion

It helps me to learn by reading closed captions for new words that I have never heard of.

As the mother of a deaf teenager, I feel it will help him increase his vocabulary and have a better understanding of the hearing world.

Captioned TV aimed at young children motivates them to read and to enjoy reading.

My daughter is more "with it" with her hearing friends.

These spontaneous comments written by parents of hearing-impaired children and by hearing-impaired adults are typical of those received daily by NCI since closed captioning began in March 1980. They are indicative of the service's impact on the lives of hearing-impaired Americans of all ages and its potential for significant contributions to their educational achievement and their psychosocial well-being in years to come.

BIBLIOGRAPHY

BALL, J.E.D. Closed captioning: The technology of today. *i.f.,* Summer 1980, pp. 15-17.

BALL, J.E.D. Television speaks to deaf Americans. Audio Engineering Society reprint #1716 (I-Z), October 1980.

BALL, J.E.D. The visual voice. *The Lion,* April 1980, pp. 6-9.

BOLTON, B. (Ed.). *Psychology of deafness for rehabilitation counselors.* Baltimore: University Park Press, 1976.

CALDWELL, D.C. The line 21 system: Closed-captioned television for hearing-impaired viewers. *Media Information Australia,* February 1981, pp. 56-60.

CALDWELL, D.C. Quota shatters silence through closed-captioned television. *Quotarian,* May 1980, pp. 3-5.

CALDWELL, D.C. Use of graded captions with instructional television for deaf learners. *American Annals of the Deaf,* 1973, *118*(4), 500-507.

CRONIN, B.J. Closed-captioned television: Today and tomorrow. *American Annals of the Deaf,* 1980, *125*(6), 726-728.

DAVIS, H., & SILVERMAN, S.R. (Eds.). *Hearing and deafness* (4th ed.). New York: Holt, Rinehart, & Winston, 1978.

FELLENDORF, G.W. (Ed.). *Bibliography on deafness* (Rev. ed.). Washington, DC: Alexander Graham Bell Assn. for the Deaf, 1976.

FRISINA, R. *A bicentennial monograph on hearing impairment: Trends in the USA.* Washington, DC: Alexander Graham Bell Assn. for the Deaf, 1976.

GETSON, P. Captioning methodologies for enhanced reading level and vocabulary development. Washington, DC: Model Secondary School for the Deaf, Gallaudet College, 1979. (mimeographed)

GUNNERSON, V.F. The silent screen. *Pacific Coaster,* December 1980, pp. 10-12.

HARDY, R.E., & CULL, G. (Eds.). *Educational and psychosocial aspects of deafness.* Springfield, IL: Charles C Thomas, 1974.

HERBER, H.L. *Teaching reading in content areas.* Englewood Cliffs, NJ: Prentice-Hall, 1970.

JENSEMA, C., & FITZGERALD, M. Background and initial audience characteristics of the closed-caption television system. *American Annals of the Deaf,* 1981, *126*(1), 32-36.

LEVINE, E.S. *The psychology of deafness.* New York: Columbia University Press, 1960.

MINDEL, E.D., & VERNON, M. *They grow in silence.* Silver Spring, MD: National Association of the Deaf, 1971.

MYKLEBUST, H.R. *The psychology of deafness* (2nd ed.). New York: Grune & Stratton, 1964.

ROSENBLOOM, B. Guidelines to writing or rewriting materials for deaf students with special emphasis on syntax. Washington, DC: Model Secondary School for the Deaf, Gallaudet College, 1979. (mimeographed)

SCHEIN, J.D., & DELK, M.T., Jr. *The deaf population of the United States.* Silver Spring, MD: National Association of the Deaf, 1974.

SMITH, F. *Understanding reading* (2nd ed.). New York: Holt, Rinehart, & Winston, 1978.

TORR, D.V. Captioning project evaluation: Final report. Washington, DC: Gallaudet College Office of Educational Technology, 1974. (mimeographed)

WITHROW, F. Educational technology and the future. *American Annals of the Deaf,* 1974, *119*(5), 605-607.

Real-Time Graphic Display and Language Development for the Hearing Impaired

4

IIIIIIIIIIIIIIIIIIIIIIIIIIIIIIIIIIIIIIIIIIIIIIIIIIIIIIIIIIIIIIIIIIIIIIIIIIIIIIIIIIIIIIIIIII

E. Ross Stuckless

A good deal is known about the development of language in most children, including the fundamental importance of hearing in this process. Parents and teachers of hearing-impaired children are particularly attuned to the importance of hearing since they can attest to what its deprivation can mean for the acquisition of spoken and written language and for lifelong communication skills.

Unfortunately for the profoundly and severely deaf child, vision is a poor substitute for hearing in the acquisition of English because, like most languages, English is most frequently spoken and transmitted through sound.

Generally, this problem has been addressed in three ways: 1) amplification and auditory training to enable the hearing-impaired child to make optimum use of the hearing which remains; 2) intensive language instruction focusing on English structure and vocabulary; and/or 3) introduction of manual communication to the child. These three general approaches are not mutually exclusive in their application. Indeed all three and their variations are used with many, and probably most, profoundly and severely deaf children in special classes throughout the United States today (Jensema & Trybus, 1978).

The thesis of this article is that a fourth approach, in the form of what might be called "real-time graphic display," is about to emerge due largely to the exploitation of current technology. This approach is viewed as augmenting, perhaps dramatically, the several approaches presently in use, particularly with the deaf child.

Real-time graphic display is the presentation of language in printed or written form to one person as it is being generated orthographically or through speech by another. An old but still practical application of real-time graphic display for many deaf people is the exchange of written notes with persons such as sales clerks (Schein, 1968) and fellow workers in the employment setting (Schein & Delk, 1974). Technological advances now

Dr. Stuckless is a professor and Director of the Office for Integrative Research at the National Technical Institute for the Deaf in Rochester, New York.

allow deaf persons to converse in real time while miles apart through the use of a telecommunication device for the deaf (TDD) which incorporates a keyboard and print display linked to the regular telephone. A third example, still some time in the future, will be computerized near-instant conversion of spoken English into readable print.

To understand why real-time graphic display holds such promise for the language development of deaf children, and perhaps others, it is important first to recognize some of the traditional distinctions between spoken and graphic communication, and second, to understand something of how language is processed through the eye and the ear.

Spoken and Graphic Communication

With few exceptions, receptive communication in English involves either a spoken or graphic medium; we listen or we read. The most evident distinction between the two is that spoken communication ipso facto generally calls upon speaking and listening, while graphic communication calls on a motor activity such as writing or typing together with the visually mediated activity called reading.

A second major distinction is that spoken communication is essentially a "real-time" medium. Most people can encode and decode spoken English at rates of 200 words per minute or more, and its transmission from one person to another is virtually instantaneous. This, together with other features, makes spoken communication ideal for live, face-to-face interaction and, since the invention of the telephone, at great distances. Traditionally, graphic communication has not shared these characteristics. Its production is limited to the speed of writing or typing. If intended for quantity distribution it must be reproduced (e.g., printed in a book), after which it must be transported physically from one place and person to another by mail or some other delivery service. At least until very recently, graphic communication could not be considered a "real-time" medium, and for this reason among others, has not been conducive to the kind of live interaction (e.g., conversation) afforded by spoken communication.

A third distinction is that, unlike graphic communication, spoken communication is transient in time. At least until the advent of the audio recorder, no permanent record of spoken communication could be retained unless it was transcribed into writing or print. Graphic communication, on the other hand, is independent of time. Although written or printed English, like spoken English, involves sequence, it is a sequence bound not by time but by space. In short, spoken communication is a "temporal-sequential" activity, while graphic communication is a "spatial-sequential" activity (Stuckless, 1978). On the surface this difference may seem to be minor, but it has major implications for English language development among children who must depend more on vision than on hearing for the acquisition of English.

Visual Processing of Language

Information received through hearing can be placed "on hold" for up to several seconds before it is actively processed by the mind. This temporary storage, called "echoic memory," permits people to retain a series of sounds in their temporal sequence long enough to process them as complete words and even sentences (Hirsh, 1975; Neisser, 1967).

Vision has its counterpart called "iconic memory" (Averbach & Coriell, 1961; Crowder, 1972) which has an advantage over echoic memory in that it can hold more information. Unfortunately, however, it has a much briefer decay time, usually about 200 milliseconds. That is to say, if the information placed in iconic memory is not actively processed by the brain within about one-fifth of a second, it is lost. For this reason, its utility for storing information in temporal sequence is quite limited.

But while the eye is a poor substitute for the ear in the reception of temporal-sequential information as conveyed by speech, the eye is well suited to the processing of spatial-sequential information as conveyed by print. Most of the research on the visual processing of temporal-sequential and spatial-sequential information has been with normally hearing subjects. However a number of investigations have also been conducted with hearing-impaired persons (Odom & Blanton, 1967; Olson & Furth, 1966; Pollard, 1977). These studies all support the conclusion that the hearing impaired, like normally hearing persons, are better able to process visual-sequential tasks when the elements are presented simultaneously in space rather than in temporal sequence.

Stuckless and Pollard (1977) compared the ability of hearing-impaired students to process fingerspelled sentences (a temporal-sequential task) and printed sentences (a spatial-sequential task). All were students of the Rochester School for the Deaf, home of the "Rochester Method" which makes extensive use of fingerspelling. The printed sentences were more readily processed than the fingerspelled sentences, although the differences were less apparent among students who had superior English skills than among students with weaker skills. Dawson (1979) has reported generally similar findings among a group of hearing-impaired children in England.

Gates (1971), using a television display, compared the ability of a group of hearing-impaired college students to visually process information through speechreading (without sound), manual communication, and print. Print conveyed more information than either of the other communication modes. Norwood (1976) and Propp (1972) have reported similar findings among deaf children and adults.

Norwood (1976) examined the relative ability of deaf adults to process captioned and interpreted news on television. Captions were more readily processed and were also preferred by deaf adults across a spectrum of English literacy levels. In this regard, it is notable that, regardless of their proficiency in speechreading and/or manual communication, most deaf people agree that captions are superior to oral/manual interpreting for conveying verbal information on television.

It might be speculated that, since the deaf child depends on vision to process temporal-sequential information (e.g., speechreading, finger-spelling), there may be a "practice effect," that is, he or she may have developed compensating strategies leading to superior skills for processing temporal-sequential information visually. However, several investigations suggest that the reverse may hold. Olson and Furth (1966), Withrow (1968), and Pollard (1977) have all reported superior performance by normally hearing subjects over hearing-impaired subjects on a number of visual temporal-sequential tasks. Withrow has speculated that the experience of normally hearing persons in processing temporal-sequential information through audition may transfer to visual processing.

However, the literature in this regard is not conclusive. Zakia and Haber (1971) have reported that hearing-impaired college students were superior to their normally hearing peers at visually processing meaningful words (in contrast to nonsense words) when the letters were presented in rapid temporal sequence. Parenthetically, they also noted that among the hearing-impaired subjects, performance on this task correlated quite highly (.70) with fluency in reading fingerspelling.

It is likely that the ability of the deaf person to visually process spoken and fingerspelled English "at the front end" (i.e., before meaning is attached) is largely a function of that person's present level of English mastery. If so, this suggests to the author that we should not depend on the visual processing of speech or fingerspelling to carry the major burden of "initiating" English. Their value to the deaf child for both language development and functional communication is probably incremental based in large measure on the level of English competence which already exists.

Since the late 1960s, Signed English and its variations (Bornstein, 1973) have received considerable attention as a visual representation of English. However, relatively little is known about the processing of signs either as a temporal-sequential or spatial-sequential activity, and perhaps it is neither. In spite of substantial research, the relationship of signing to English acquisition remains conjectural (Stuckless, 1976a, 1976b). Recent work on the use of English markers by children exposed to Signed English indicates that the use of such markers by children does not necessarily follow from their use by teachers (Bornstein & Saulnier, 1981). This leads the present author to ask how, or indeed the extent to which, these markers are being processed (or attended to) by the child who does not already have an English foundation.

Traditional Print

Unlike speech and other temporal-sequential communication media, print as used in books, newspapers, etc., has a static, time-free quality. Because of its permanence, we are generally able to read at our own pace, focusing on a word or group of words as long as necessary for processing. Contrary to popular belief, our eyes are stationary most of the time as we read. On the average, our eyes are in motion only 6% of the time, 94% of the time being spent in fixation pauses (Tinker, 1965). During this fixation, the same image can be entered repeatedly into iconic memory as often as necessary for it to be recognized. Thus, although linguistic sequence is retained in reading just as in listening to spoken language, the elements are glued together by space rather than by time. For example, this paragraph remains on the page to be read again, if necessary. If presented orally, it would have been lost because we would have proceeded to another point.

However, while print is conducive to visual processing of language, it would be foolish to think that the only necessity to establish English in young deaf children is to surround them with books and make them read. Many of us have heard others say, "Deaf people must be very good readers because they depend so much on seeing." We know, of course, that one does not follow directly from the other.

But why not? The simple answer is that processing of print goes well beyond eye fixation and iconic memory. It depends on being able to attach meaning which in turn depends on a repertoire of existing language experiences and skills. By language we mean both its vocabulary and its structure. Scholars struggled for centuries to decipher the characters of ancient hieroglyphics, but it was not until the Rosetta stone was unearthed that meaning could be attached. The normally hearing child has his or her own "Rosetta stone" in the form of spoken language. The young hearing-impaired child may not, and if prelingually and profoundly deaf, probably does not.

Real-Time Graphic Display

Early in this article, several distinctions were drawn between spoken and graphic communication as traditionally used. But today, due to technological advances those distinctions are in the process of breaking down, and the long-standing advantages of each, as well as some of the disadvantages, are beginning to merge.

Conversion of Speech into Print. The traditional dichotomy between speaking/listening and reading/writing is beginning to fade. More advances have been made in converting printed language into "machine voice" or "speech synthesis" than in converting spoken language into print. This is for the simple reason that it is much easier to teach a machine to recognize print than to recognize spoken language. The former represents a major breakthrough for blind persons, reducing their dependence on braille and live readers. However, the useful applications for deaf persons are probably quite limited. If a deaf person's speech is unintelligible to the "untrained ear," he or she has recourse to writing and increasingly, with growing numbers of normally hearing persons who can sign, to signs or fingerspelling.

A major breakthrough being awaited for deaf children and adults is the automatic computer-based recognition of spoken language and its near-instantaneous conversion into print. Houde (1979) has discussed the current state of the art and, like others before him, projected that fully functional applications for deaf people lie at least 10 years distant, not because of technology per se, but because of the extreme complexity of spoken language. One major obstacle is the fact that while people separate printed words in a sentence with spaces, they do not typically pause between each word when speaking. The automatic recognition by computers of discrete spoken words and their conversion into print is now a limited reality. Automatic recognition of language as normally spoken is not. However, it will come, and when it does, the deaf child will have greater access to language whenever it is spoken in his or her presence.

In the meantime, there have been many other developments of an intermediate nature, all of which require a human "transcriber." Captioned films and captioned television are two primary examples. The closed captioning of television warrants particular attention for the number of hours each week captions are available, for its variety in programming and range of appeal for children and adults, and particularly for the fact that it is now in many homes, reaching even the preschool child. As of June 1980, over 20,000 closed caption adapters had been purchased for home use by an estimated 48,000 hearing-impaired viewers, among whom 25% are estimated to be of preschool and school age (Jensema & Fitzgerald, 1981).

Increasing numbers of hearing-impaired children and young adults are now receiving much of their education in integrated classroom settings. This has brought added attention to manual and oral interpreting of speech. It has also brought attention to the importance of class notes using voluntary or paid notetakers to convert speech into "hard copy" (Osguthorpe, Long, & Ellsworth, 1980; Stuckless, 1969). There is also some exploratory interest in the use of a stenotypist to transcribe speech into its phonetic components which would then be fed into a computer and emerge for the student to read verbatim on a screen while also furnishing the student with hard copy. Most of the technology necessary for this procedure is similar to that of real-time captioning of television which is presently under development (McCoy & Shumway, 1979).

Real-Time Print. It was indicated early in the article that graphic communication, unlike speech, lacks immediacy in time. It must be physically packaged and forwarded. But again due to technology, this is changing, and print is increasingly becoming a real-time mode. As it approaches real time, it also takes on more of the characteristics of spoken language as an interactive, conversational medium.

There can be little doubt that the telecommunication device for the deaf or TDD (Castle, 1981) is among technology's greatest direct contributions to hearing-impaired people. Today, there are at least 13 manufacturers of TDDs and the number in use by hearing-impaired people is estimated to be 40,000 or more. The TDD transmits print between two users at the same rate as the standard telephone transmits speech, limited only by the users' speed and skill in typing.

We are witnessing greatly expanded uses of computers and computer technology to aid in communication with other people. In the New England area there is a network of deaf households linked by computer terminals and a computer permitting both live interaction and broader computer use such as an "Electronic Mailbox" (Cerf, 1978; Strassler, 1980). Watson (1979) has described other applications of the computer to real-time graphic display and interaction, including the TICCIT system which is in use at the Model Secondary School for the Deaf at Gallaudet College in Washington, D.C.

All these developments and others are giving graphic communication an immediacy in time not hitherto possible, and with this immediacy in time, the potential for live conversation.

Transience of Real-Time Print. A major attribute of graphic communication, in contrast to spoken communication, has been its relative permanence. However, as print is brought into real time, by definition it begins to take on a temporal, transient quality which could in turn act against effective visual processing which was discussed earlier. Virtually no attention was given to reading rate among deaf children and adults until the introduction of captioned film and captioned television (Braverman & Hertzog, 1980; Shroyer & Birch, 1980). Because of the need to synchronize captions with the flow of the dialogue's sound, some control of reading rate had to be removed from the reader and placed in the hands of the person responsible for the captioning, as well as the original speaker. Other hitherto unnecessary questions have also come to the fore; for example, how many characters to the line and how many lines on the screen at one time for optimum reading.

In the interest of compactness and portability, some TDDs use Times Square-type graphic displays which move across a screen and disappear rather than a hard copy print, introducing a temporal-sequential element which may be satisfactory for the deaf person with good English skills but unsatisfactory for others. Present and future technology for real-time graphic display for deaf children and adults should not be permitted to outstrip their ability to process language visually.

Implications for Language Development

Most children learn the basic language of their families well before they enter school. This is evident not only in the spoken language of normally hearing children, but also in the signed language of deaf children of signing deaf parents. The author is unaware of any literature on the English language development of deaf children within homes where print has been used consistently for communication.

We now come to the question of what if a deaf child were regularly presented with print which had the same real-time quality as spoken language? What if the deaf child could literally read the conversation at the dinner table? What if, when the mother was dressing the young child, this child could see in print, "Let's put on your socks," at the same time the words were uttered? What if, as the teacher was speaking to the class, his or her spoken language could also be displayed on a screen in print? In this connection, the author and a cooperating teacher of the hearing impaired conducted a pilot study in which during part of each school day over a 3-month period the teacher spoke and typed simultaneously, the print appearing on a television screen. Students responded in speech and finger-spelling. Although the pilot study did not permit conclusions about English gains, the approach did sustain the attention and interest of the students over the 3-month period.

What if the deaf child or adult had access in the home to 20 hours or more a week of print synchronized to the spoken language and actions of cartoons and other real-time events on television? With closed captioning this has become a reality. Will these and other applications of real-time graphic display converge to enhance and even initiate English language development in the deaf child?

Not alone. Again, real-time graphic display has the potential of *augmenting,* perhaps dramatically, the several approaches presently in use, particularly with the profoundly deaf child. Real-time graphic display per se will not provide the deaf child with the opportunity for expression and verbal interaction. This is generally inherent in language development, at least in one's first language. Even if not essential, it would leave the child with only receptive language or half a communication system.

It follows that the young deaf child must also have a means of expression which real-time graphic display will not provide. We cannot expect the deaf child at age 2 and 3 to express himself or herself graphically by writing or typing. By the same token, it is the exceptional profoundly deaf child who has functional speaking skills at the same age. A third option lies in manual expression *if* it reinforces English. It is not the intent of the author to urge one above the other. For most young profoundly deaf children he is persuaded that all three are in the interest of English language development, although not necessarily simultaneously at a particular stage in the child's early development. In point of fact, there is little research to guide us on this latter question.

Real-time graphic display will also not obviate the need for formal language instruction. The author is optimistic, however, that it could lead to an altered language curriculum which, as for normally hearing children, focuses more on enriching than on establishing language. If so, implications would extend beyond language instruction itself. First, a greater portion of the school day could be dedicated to other much-needed areas of learning, and second, with an English foundation, deaf children could make much greater general education progress.

This all sounds rather futuristic, but much of the technology for real-time graphic display is with us today, some of it waiting to be fully exploited for the benefit of children who must depend heavily upon vision for language learning.

REFERENCES

AVERBACH, E., & CORIELL, A.S. Short-term memory in vision. *Bell System Technical Journal,* 1961, *40,* 309-328.

BORNSTEIN, H. A description of some current sign systems designed to represent English. *American Annals of the Deaf,* 1973, *118* (3), 454-463.

BORNSTEIN, H., & SAULNIER, K. Signed English: A brief follow-up to the first evaluation. *American Annals of the Deaf,* 1981, *126* (1), 69-72.

BRAVERMAN, B., & HERTZOG, M. The effects of caption rate and language level on comprehension of a captioned video presentation. *American Annals of the Deaf,* 1980, *125* (7), 943-948.

CASTLE, D.L. *Telecommunication training for the deaf.* Rochester, NY: National Technical Institute for the Deaf, 1981.

CERF, V. The electronic mailbox: A new communication tool for the hearing impaired. *American Annals of the Deaf,* 1978, *123* (5), 768-772.

CRANDALL, K. Inflectional morphemes in the manual English of young hearing-impaired children and their mothers. *Journal of Speech and Hearing Research,* 1978, *21* (2), 372-386.

CROWDER, R.G. Visual auditory memory. In J.F. Kavanagh & I.G. Mattingly (Eds.), *Language by ear and by eye.* Cambridge: MIT Press, 1972.

DAWSON, E.H. *Cognitive functioning of prelingually deaf children.* Unpublished doctoral dissertation, University of Durham, England, 1979.

GATES, R. The reception of verbal information by deaf students through a television medium: A comparison of speechreading, manual communication, and reading. *Proceedings of the Convention of American Instructors of the Deaf,* Little Rock, 1971, 513-522.

HIRSH, I.J. Temporal aspects of hearing. In D.B. Tower (Ed.), *Human communication and its disorders.* New York: Raven Press, 1975.

HOUDE, B. Prospects for automatic recognition of speech. *American Annals of the Deaf,* 1979, *124* (5), 568-572.

JENSEMA, C., & FITZGERALD, M. Background and initial audience characteristics of the closed-caption television system. *American Annals of the Deaf,* 1981, *126* (1), 32-36.

JENSEMA, C., & TRYBUS, R. *Communication patterns and educational achievement of hearing-impaired students.* Washington, DC: Office of Demographic Studies, Gallaudet College, Series T, Nov. 2, 1978.

McCoy, E., & Shumway, R. Real-time captioning — promise for the future. *American Annals of the Deaf,* 1979, *124* (5), 681-690.

Neisser, U. *Cognitive psychology.* New York: Appleton–Century–Crofts, 1967.

Norwood, M. *Comparison of an interpreted and a captioned newscast among deaf high school graduates and deaf college graduates.* Unpublished doctoral dissertation, University of Maryland, 1976.

Odom, P.B., & Blanton, R.L. Rule learning in deaf and hearing subjects. *American Journal of Psychology,* 1967, *80,* 391-397.

Olson, J.E., & Furth, H.G. Visual memory-span in the deaf. *American Journal of Psychology,* 1966, *79,* 480-484.

Osguthorpe, R.T., Long, G.L., & Ellsworth, R.G. The effects of reviewing class notes for deaf and hearing students. *American Annals of the Deaf,* 1980, *125* (5), 554-558.

Pollard, G.W. *Information processing in two presentation modes by deaf and hearing subjects.* Unpublished doctoral dissertation, University of Illinois, 1977.

Propp, G. *An experimental study on the encoding of verbal information for visual transmission to the hearing-impaired learner.* Unpublished doctoral dissertation, University of Nebraska, 1972.

Schein, J. *The deaf community: Studies in the social psychology of deafness.* Washington, DC: Gallaudet College, 1968.

Schein, J., & Delk, M. *The deaf population of the United States.* Silver Spring, MD: National Association of the Deaf, 1974.

Shroyer, E.H., & Birch, J.W. Captions and reading rates of hearing-impaired students. *American Annals of the Deaf,* 1980, *125* (7), 916-922.

Strassler, B. Telecom and you: The ASCII–Baudot dilemma. *The Silent News,* March 1980.

Stuckless, E.R. *A notetaking procedure for deaf students in regular classes.* Occasional Papers No. 1, National Technical Institute for the Deaf, 1969.

Stuckless, E.R. An interpretive review of research on manual communication in the education of deaf children: Language development and information transmission. In P. Henderson (Ed.), *Methods of communication currently used in the education of deaf children.* London: Royal National Institute for the Deaf, 1976. (a)

Stuckless, E.R. Manual and graphic communication. In R. Frisina (Ed.), *A bicentennial monograph on hearing impairment: Trends in the U.S.A.* Washington, DC: A.G. Bell Assn. for the Deaf, 1976. (b)

Stuckless, E.R. Technology and the visual processing of verbal information by deaf people. *American Annals of the Deaf,* 1978, *123* (6), 630-636.

Stuckless, E.R., & Pollard, G.W. Processing of fingerspelling and print by deaf students. *American Annals of the Deaf,* 1977, *122* (5), 475-479.

Tinker, M.A. *Bases for effective reading.* Minneapolis: University of Minnesota Press, 1965.

Watson, P. The utilization of the computer with the hearing impaired and the handicapped. *American Annals of the Deaf,* 1979, *124* (5), 670-680.

Withrow, F.B. Intermediate memory span of deaf and normally hearing children. *Exceptional Children,* 1968, *35*(1), 33-41.

Zakia, R.D., & Haber, R.N. Sequential letter and word recognition in deaf and hearing subjects. *Perception and Psychophysics,* 1971, *9* (1B), 111-114.

Speech Technology and Communication for the Hearing Impaired 5

IIIIIIIIIIIIIIIIIIIIIIIIIIIIIIIIIIIIIIIIIIIIIIIIIIIIIIIIIIIIIIIIIIIIIIIIIIIIIIIIIIIIIIIIIIIIII

J.M. Pickett

T he electronic industry is rapidly developing new speech technology for a variety of communication needs. For example, there are small computers that recognize spoken zip codes to direct mail on to conveyer belts (Martin & Welch, 1980). In still another application, a major group of mutual funds offers a telephone service for automatic information response upon recognizing digits spoken by the inquirer. This system can recognize any of the 10 digits as spoken by anyone. In addition to such commercial uses of speech technology, educational uses are made of artificial speech synthesized electronically from typed-in instructions; examples are the Texas Instrument's Speak 'n Spell and the HandiVoice made by HC Electronics for the non-oral handicapped.

Speech technology will continue to grow because there are many everyday transactions that would become more economical and convenient through automatic speech recognition and automatic response by voice from stored symbols. These developments have a great potential for widening telephone communication by the deaf.

Thus far, the major research efforts in aids to speech for the deaf have concentrated on visual or tactile substitutes for hearing. This approach has a long history, but the discussion below will be limited to the potentials of newer developments, visual indicators of speech, and wearable tactile aids for reception.

Speech technology can also be applied in totally new types of hearing aids. For example, one type would enhance those speech patterns which are distorted or obscured by partial deafness. Another new type of aid attempts to provide hearing by electrical stimulation of the auditory nerve.

This then is the field of potential new aids for speech communication: visible speech, tactile reception of speech, electrical hearing, and signal enhancement. In addition, the technologies of artificial speech, automatic speech recognition, and computer-modeling of speech can be made useful to the hearing impaired. The field is extremely broad, and we can only briefly present here what has already been done and what needs to be

Dr. Pickett is director of the Sensory Communication Research Laboratory, Research Division, Gallaudet College in Washington, D.C.

accomplished. (For detailed discussions and descriptions of the past and present work see Levitt, Pickett, & Houde 1980).

Speech-Training Aids and Tactile Speech

Visible Speech.   Speech technology is based on microprocessors that analyze incoming speech into its components. The components are different sound frequencies, each of which has a different amplitude value. The pattern of amplitudes across the frequencies is called the sound spectrum. In speech these spectrum patterns vary in time with the sequence of different articulations of the speaker as he or she moves his or her tongue and lips to form the different consonants and vowels. For a speech aid, the complete spectrogram pattern — the picture of the spectrum changes in time — may be instantly displayed on a standard video monitor.* Alternatively, selected features of the spectrum may be displayed using simple on-off indicators, as in the Upton Eyeglass Speechreader (see below). Speech Spectrographic Display (SSD) instant spectrograms are being tested for use in speech-training programs with deaf students at the Rochester School for the Deaf and at the National Technical Institute for the Deaf.

In Japan, a color TV receiver is being used in an experimental speech trainer under development at Kumamoto University. The three color-channels of the TV transmission are controlled by three selected features of the spectrum of the voiced portions of the speech signal (i.e., the vowels and semivowels). These three spectrum features vary with the vocal tract shape and thus their color indications may be useful for teaching the movements of the vocal tract that produce normal speech.

In contrast to the SSD and the color TV speech trainer, the Upton Eyeglass Speechreader is a speech display designed primarily as an aid to speech reception. It is a very simple, wearable system (see Figure 1) in which the display segments are only lighted one at any time. Although the display indications of the speech-sound categories are far from error-free, some information of modest consistency is better than no information at all. Improved reception over speechreading alone was demonstrated in tests carried out in the author's laboratory and by tests on the inventor of the system, a hearing-impaired engineer. The Upton system is ready to field-test, after a few design improvements, but currently there is no such project underway. It will be found useful primarily by late-deafened persons who lead lives requiring extensive speech communication.

Tactile Speech.   The sound patterns of speech can be presented on the skin as well as to the eye. The use of the skin would have advantages, especially in an aid for the deaf child where it might be difficult to control

---

*The best current example is the SSD (Speech Spectrographic Display) of Spectraphonics, Inc.

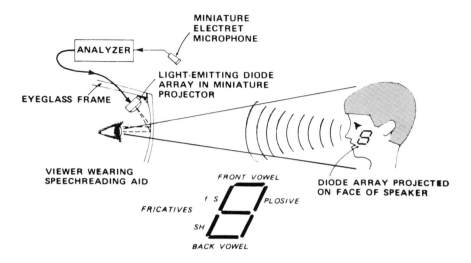

Figure 1. The Upton Eyeglass Speechreader system. The microphone and analyzer, worn by the hearing-impaired user, control activation of the red light-bars in a standard alphanumeric array of LEDs which are mounted as a small "projector" at the corner of the eyeglass frame. The lights are aimed at a tiny reflecting area on the rear surface of the eyeglass lens. The image of the light-bars appears in space before the wearer and can be placed in line with the person speaking. Each element is lighted only one at a time to indicate a sound pattern correlated with a class of speech sounds, as noted on the enlarged LED pattern.

visual attention. Work on this is being done at the Smith-Kettlewell Institute by Frank Saunders and at the Mailman Center by Kimbrough Oller.

A good tactile speech translator is extremely important because it would be the best hope for normal spoken language development by the deaf child if the system can be wearable and fitted early. The tactile approach has particular potential for the deaf child to provide continuous reception and self-monitoring of speech. The ideal wearable tactile aid would support the acquisition of spoken language by a totally deaf child (Goldstein & Stark, 1976). However, compared with vision, the tactile sense is not very well understood. Thus, basic research on tactile coding is needed, as well as further technical development of speech-decoding especially designed for the skin.

Speech Movement Indicators. There are some interesting new devices for indicating the positions and movements of the tongue and larynx in order to train and correct the speech of the hearing impaired. Such devices may operate from the speech received or more directly from the tongue or lips themselves.

If the speech signal is used alone, then its spectrum must be transformed into the normal vocal tract shape that would result in that spectrum. This is done by locating certain features of the spectrum and then determining a reasonable tract shape that would produce those features. The tract shape is then displayed as a curve representing the cross-sectional area of the vocal tract. The analysis and display are virtually instantaneous and "movements of the tongue" appear on the screen as the trainee speaks. Such a system is being tested at Cambridge University in England (Crichton, Fallside, & Eng, 1974; also reprinted in Levitt et al., 1980).

Speech indicators that respond directly to articulation and phonation have also been developed. These are often laboratory sensors, originally developed for research on speech movements, that have been adapted for speech training by the addition of a suitable display. An example is the artificial palate which holds an array of many electrical contacts in the mouth. Contacts of the tongue are then signaled on a display. The contact shape and areas of the trainee's tongue can be seen, thus providing feedback about a very important, but invisible, articulator. Research with the palate system as a speech trainer is carried out by Samuel Fletcher at the University of Alabama-Birmingham. A Japanese group has developed and used a similar trainer system manufactured by Rion Co., Ltd., called the Electro-Palatograph. Fletcher has also developed a tongue-distance display.

Another direct sensor is the Laryngograph. It responds to phonation of the vocal folds by monitoring the degree of contact between the vocal folds. During voice production, the vocal folds move back and forth very rapidly, closing and opening, to modulate the airflow from the lungs, thereby producing the fundamental source-sound for the voice. The rapidly changing configurations of the contact between the folds determine the person's voice characteristics. The contact configurations result in a periodic wave derived by the Laryngograph. This wave is then processed to yield, for display, the voice pitch, the timing of voice onset relative to the upper articulations, and possibly, normalness of voice quality (Fourcin & Abberton, 1971). Abberton, Parker, and Fourcin (1977) developed and tested some procedures for Laryngograph display in training of the voice pitch and rhythm of deaf persons.

Electro-Auditory Implants for Hearing

Sensations of sound can be elicited by electrical stimulation of the auditory nerve with weak currents. There are several research programs designed either to study methods of stimulation for such a prosthesis or to fit existing prostheses and train patients in their use. This research and its historical background are described in detail in Levitt et al. (1980) and in McPherson and Davis (1978). Here we provide only a brief summary of the very complex and controversial situation of developments for "electrical hearing," also referred to as cochlear implants.

In one approach, stimulating electrodes are implanted surgically in the cochlea of the deaf patient (usually a case of sudden late profound deafness). When the implanted electrode is activated with a sufficient current that is a replica of speech waves, the patient hears sound, but it is not intelligible. Nevertheless, patients report daily experiences of personal satisfaction with the sound they receive even though it is heard as noises and buzzes that have little or no similarity to the original sound input.

The basic reason for the nonspeech character of the electro-auditory sound is that simply to apply the sound wave of speech to the electrode does not simulate the normal sound-to-nerve processing. This processing does not normally produce a sound wave on the auditory nerve because nerve units respond only in discrete equal pulses, not in a wave-like fashion. The transformation from sound wave to nerve impulses is only partially understood even for the simplest types of sound inputs, let alone for the highly complex sounds of speech. It is not likely that the full knowledge necessary for electronic simulation of the normal auditory neural processing will soon be available for application to the needed implants.

However, it is known that the frequency-dimension of input sounds is represented to some degree by the successive places along the length of the basilar membrane where correspondingly different fanned-out fibers of the auditory nerve connect. Thus, if electrical stimulation could be properly arrayed over this succession of nerve endings, some type of frequency representation or discrimination might be found useful. Therefore multiple-electrode implants have been developed by several research groups. Encouraging results were recently reported by a group in Australia (Tong, Clark, Seligman, & Patrick, 1980). In tests with an implanted patient, their 10-electrode system was found to provide some useful discrimination of certain important speech features that are virtually impossible to discriminate by speechreading. In reception of simple sentences, the patient obtained a score of 76% correct speechreading with the system vs. 22% without it.

A physiological question that has been raised concerns the long-term viability of artificial nerve stimulation. It is not yet known how the auditory nerve fibers will tolerate artificial stimulation, for how long, or whether a decline in their sensitivity will develop. These questions are under study in experiments with animals.

Because of the complexities and unknowns of the cochlear approach, one group of workers in Britain has developed a less invasive electrical stimulator system (Douek, Fourcin, Moore, & Clarke, 1977). It has the limitation of providing only one channel of stimulation, but nevertheless may be the most useful approach for widespread adoption at present since the surgery and electrical processing are rather simple. A single electrode is led in under the skin of the ear canal to cross the middle ear and rest on the promontory. The electrode is activated only with the basic voice pitch component of received speech with no attempt to represent the middle and upper components. It is known that the auditory system will respond with a heard pitch proportional to the frequency of the fundamental voice pitch. Voice pitch alone is known to be a valuable aid to speechreading, because it helps to separate the run-together appearance of words and phrases. Thus, the system of Douek et al. attempts only to provide voice pitch sensations as an aid to speechreading and voice control. This system has a good chance for current success because the surgery is simple and reversible. The main unknown factor is the amount of benefit from the representation of voice pitch that will be experienced by different persons.

Obviously the ultimate goal should be a neuro-electrical simulation of hearing natural speech, but its attainment appears to lie far in the future.

Speech-Computing for the Hearing Impaired

Artificial Speech and Speech Recognition Systems. Technologies for automatic speech recognition and synthesis of sentences have potentially useful applications for the hearing impaired. If these technologies can be successfully applied, the oral communication community for profoundly deaf persons can be greatly expanded. Deaf persons who cannot speak intelligibly could produce speech messages by typing into their synthesizers; their normally hearing correspondents could reply, speaking into a central speech recognizer which would then send a written version of the spoken message to the deaf person's teletype. The synthesis of intelligible speech from a typed input has developed to the point of commercial feasibility as seen, for example, in the portable speech synthesizer, the HandiVoice, a product developed by the Votrax Division of Federal Screw Works and made by HC Electronics. HandiVoice and other synthesizers are currently used by nonvocal, normally hearing persons (Carlson, Galyas, Granström, Petersson, & Zacharisson, 1980; Fant, Galyas, Branderud, Svenson, & McAllister, 1976; National Research Council, 1977), but they might not be used by those deaf persons who do not have intelligible speech.

Systems have been developed that successfully recognize spoken words and phrases if these are suitably constrained. The present constraints are on size of vocabulary, number of different speakers, and the requirement that excessive noise should be avoided. Also, the systems must be given some experience with the speakers. Not just any unknown speaker can have anything he or she says recognized correctly, but if the users are well known and if they deal with a restricted topic or activity, recognition can be usefully accurate. This capability could expand current use of TTY telephones to include voice-only telephone correspondents who might be frequently called. The correspondents would have to be known and they would have to limit themselves to constrained topics and vocabulary which could be set up by the caller's use of special code words.

General unrestricted communication through a speech recognizer may be possible with a visible speaker; the lip and tongue configurations seen on the speaker can be used to fill in those features of speech which electronic systems have difficulty in recognizing. A special recognition system of this type, called the Autocuer, has been developed and tested with trained deaf viewers by R.O. Cornett of Gallaudet College. The overall principle of operation of the Autocuer is the same as the method of Cued Speech, a manual system introduced by Cornett in 1965.

Processing Speech of the Deaf for Intelligibility. A recognition system might also be used by deaf persons to receive their own speech, recognize what they are saying, and improve intelligibility by activating a speech synthesizer to do the talking. However, recognition of the speech of the hearing impaired might be more difficult to use than a well-indexed set of phrase instructions for which codes could be typed to activate a synthesizer.

Speech recognition systems can also be applied in speech training. Suitable recognition templates are stored in the recognizer for the deaf person to practice pronouncing. In addition, a word recognizer can be programmed to act as a practice monitor. A deaf person occasionally pronounces a word or phrase very well, but most of the time he or she may not make a correct production without extended practice. The more correct productions of the individual trainee are used as a standard during practice to try to achieve consistently good production. M.J. Osberger is currently testing this concept at the Boys Town Institute for Communicative Disorders in Children in Omaha, Nebraska.

Computer-Modeling of Speech Production. Computer-modeling of the biomechanics of speech production is a special area of current speech research that is advancing very rapidly. As adequate models develop, they can be used in reverse as aids in speech training. For example, a bio-mechanical model of the vocal folds and their controlling muscles is under development (Titze & Talkin, 1979). When such a model is realized and found to be reasonably accurate, it may be used in reverse to indicate the pattern of muscle control that is responsible for an abnormal habit of phonation. Such indications could serve as displays for voice training.

Computer-modeling of the articulation movements is currently used in research on speech production. This research could develop a technology with wide applications in the study of abnormal speech. The movements in the model can be adjusted and control a synthesizer to produce the same sequence of sounds as produced by an unintelligible speaker when he or she tries to say a given phrase. Then the synthesizer's "articulation" will indicate what the speaker may be doing wrong.

Speech Signal Enhancement for Hearing Aids.   Hearing impairment causes distortions of both the frequency information and the patterning of speech in time. Electronic processing to circumvent these problems has not yet been devised and tested. This is perhaps the most challenging and complex problem of the field, primarily because the distortions themselves are not very well defined at this time. Unfortunately, we don't know exactly what distortions are imposed by the impaired ear. If we understood the distortions, it is certain that technology could be devised for hearing aids that would process incoming speech in special ways that would in effect reduce the heard distortion by enhancing certain features of speech.

The basic distortion problem is under study in various institutions, including Gallaudet College, The Massachusetts Institute of Technology, Northwestern University, The Royal Institute of Technology (Stockholm), and the British MRC Hearing Research Institute (University of Nottingham). At these places, special laboratories work on manipulating the sound patterns of speech features to make them more discriminable to the hearing impaired.

The potential here is quite extensive in that the population to be benefited is several million people in the United States alone, primarily those with moderate-to-severe, but not profound, impairments.

Computer-Processed Speech for Hearing Diagnosis.   Synthetic speech sounds from computers have been used in the author's laboratory, and some others, to gain a better understanding of the difficulties which many hearing-impaired persons experience in discriminating speech sounds, even when the sounds are amplified for optimum reception. For example, a particular transition sound was synthesized that is known to differentiate the consonants *b, d,* and *g* for normally hearing listeners. These transitions were programmed in special tests for hearing-impaired listeners. It was found that the transition discrimination of *some* impaired listeners was very poor, but could be improved by partial suppression of frequencies below the transition (Danaher, Osberger, & Pickett, 1973). A test of this type might be used in diagnosis to identify those patients who would specifically benefit from a hearing aid that suppressed the low frequency. With a synthetic speech signal, it is easy to arrange adjustments of the relative intensities of different acoustic speech features. Computer-processed speech can be used in many ways to explore discrimination of the basic cues and, in the future, aid in diagnosis for fitting speech-processing hearing aids that would enhance discrimination (Picheny, Durlach, & Braida, 1980; Revoile, Pickett, Holden, & Brandt, 1981).

REFERENCES

ABBERTON, E., PARKER, A., & FOURCIN, A. Speech improvement in deaf adults using laryngograph displays. In *Research Conference on Speech-Processing Aids for the Deaf.* Washington, DC: Gallaudet College, Sensory Communication Research Laboratory, 1977.

CARLSON, R., GALYAS, K., GRANSTRÖM, B., PETTERSSON, M., & ZACHRISSON, G. *Speech synthesis for the non-vocal in training and communication* (Speech Transmission Laboratory Quarterly Progress and Status Reports, 1/1980). Stockholm, Sweden: Royal Institute of Technology, Department of Speech Communication, 1980.

CRICHTON, R.G., FALLSIDE, F., & ENG, C. Linear prediction model of speech production with applications to deaf speech training. *Proceedings of the Institute of Electrical Engineering Control and Science,* 1974, *121,* 865-873.

DANAHER, E.M., OSBERGER, M.J., & PICKETT, J.M. Discrimination of formant frequency transitions in synthetic vowels. *Journal of Speech and Hearing Research,* 1973, *16,* 439-451.

DOUEK, E., FOURCIN, A., MOORE, B., & CLARKE, G. A new approach to the cochlear implant. *Proceedings of the Royal Society of Medicine,* 1977, *70,* 379-383.

FANT, G., GALYAS, K., BRANDERUD, P., SVENSON, S.G., & McALLISTER, R. Aids for speech-handicapped. *Scandinavian Journal of Rehabilitation Medicine,* 1976, *8,* 65-66.

FOURCIN, A., & ABBERTON, E. First applications of a new laryngograph. *Medical Biology Illus.,* 1971, *21,* 172-182.

GOLDSTEIN, M., & STARK, R. Modification of vocalizations of preschool deaf children by vibro-tactile and visual displays. *The Journal of the Acoustical Society of America,* 1976, *59,* 1477-1481.

LEVITT, H., PICKETT, J.M., & HOUDE, R. (Eds.). *Sensory aids for the hearing-impaired.* New York: IEEE Press, 1980.

MARTIN, T.B., & WELCH, J.R. Practical speech recognizers and some performance effectiveness parameters. In W.A. Lea (Ed.), *Trends in speech recognition.* Englewood Cliffs, NJ: Prentice-Hall, 1980.

McPHERSON, D.L., & DAVIS, M.S. (Eds.). *Advances in prosthetic devices for the deaf: A technical workshop.* Rochester, NY: National Technical Institute for the Deaf, 1978.

National Research Council of Canada. *Proceedings of the workshop on communication aids for the handicapped.* Ottawa, Canada: Author, 1977.

PICHENY, M.A., DURLACH, N.I., & BRAIDA, L.D. Speaking clearly: Intelligibility and acoustic characteristics of sentences. *The Journal of the Acoustical Society of America,* 1980, *67,* S38 (Suppl. 1).

REVOILE, S.G., PICKETT, J.M., HOLDEN, L.D., & BRANDT, F.D. Pitch recognition for noise bursts adjacent to a synthetic vowel for hearing-impaired listeners. Submitted for publication, 1981.

TITZE, I.R., & TALKIN, D.T. A theoretical study of the effects of various laryngeal configurations on the acoustics of phonation. *The Journal of the Acoustical Society of America,* 1979, *66,* 60-74.

TONG, Y.C., CLARK, G.M., SELIGMAN, P.M., & PATRICK, J.F. Speech processing for a multiple-electrode cochlear implant hearing prosthesis. *The Journal of the Acoustical Society of America,* 1980, *68,* 1897-1899.

Technology to Facilitate Language Acquisition 6

Margaret S. Withrow

How do children learn to use language? The ability of the infant to re-call sensory experiences and to organize them into meaningful wholes is the beginning of the cognitive process. The infant explores his or her environment through taste, touch, movement, sight, and sound. The child organizes these experiences into concepts about his or her world and eventually associates them with language symbols. In the early stages of this memory process, the young child may recall past experiences as rich sensory images of the real event. This bank of sensory imagery eventually is reduced to cues which become signs and symbols for the child's world. Language becomes the shorthand for sensory images and the most common level of conscious thought.

Normally, a child learns to listen and then to speak. Dale (1972) described language learning as a matter of hypotheses-formation and hypotheses-testing in an active process. "The child continually formulates hypotheses about underlying rules of the language he hears and tests them by attempting to use them to understand speech and also to construct his own utterances." Children develop these hypotheses even though most of the language they hear is creative (not previously heard) and, in many cases, not perfectly grammatical. In testing these hypotheses, children learn there are language rules that can be used in many situations and that can be broken.

Over the past 20 years, increased attention has been given to language development in both normal children and handicapped children by psychologists and linguists. Chomsky (1959, 1965) provided a basis for the research and interest in these disciplines. Much of the early work centered on the acquisition of syntax and was a natural consequence of Chomsky's research. Current theories and research (Bloom, 1974; Clark, 1974; Sinclair-deZwart, 1967; Slobin, 1973) have emphasized the cognitive or

Dr. Withrow is an independent educational technology consultant, residing in Washington, DC, who specializes in design and development of technology applications to learning.

conceptual development in the child in the language development process. Bloom stated:

> Understanding and speaking do not develop separately with children learning different "rules" for each. Inasmuch as communication depends upon the extent to which the semantic intention of the speaker matches the semantic interpretation of the listener, the knowledge that each has could not be independent . . . . But, while it is most probably not the case that speaking and understanding are altogether separate developments, it is by no means clear that the emergence of speech and understanding shadow each other. (p. 285)

McNeill (1970) has hypothesized that from the beginning a child has the concept of sentence and all utterances of one word or more can be described as representing one or more of the grammatical relations of a sentence. Nygren (1976) discussed the implications of this language theory for language-deficient children by noting that:

> Two capacities are necessary for learning language in the natural way. The child must have intact sensory mechanisms in order to receive the sound of the language and to experience the environment the language describes, and he or she needs the ability to generalize personal experience with language.
>
> The reason the handicapped child may not learn language spontaneously the way normal peers do is that the child lacks the sensory ability to generalize from the few critical examples of each language concept the natural situation provides.
>
> A young child who does not learn language spontaneously may appear to respond appropriately to spoken language. However, in this case the child may only be reading the situation or responding to a gesture. The question of careful assessment of the language knowledge of the child with deficient language is extremely important. While assessment goes on constantly when parents talk to young normal children, it is an informal and probably unconscious activity.
>
> For the language handicapped child, this assessment cannot be an unconscious activity. One must know how much the child is really responding to so as to provide for progress to the next level. The fact that the child will not be able to take that step independently is what distinguishes him or her from the normal child. (p. 7)

It can be assumed that success in the American school system is dependent upon the ability of the learner to communicate. What are the communication processes and barriers of hearing impairment to those processes? Because they do not hear spoken language completely, hearing-impaired children tend not to develop the comprehensive language skills of listening, speaking, reading, and writing at the same time or to the same degree of complexity as their normally hearing peers. Standard reading tests show that the average prelingually deaf adult reads at a level between the second and fourth grade, and that deaf children rarely exceed the fifth grade reading level (Furth, 1973). Moreover, even these scores may indicate higher reading ability than deaf adults find functional. Studies using the "cloze procedure"* requiring students to fill in blank grammatical

---

*The "cloze procedure" is one method of determining the ability of a child to properly use parts of language. Sentences are written that omit words or groups of words and the child is asked to fill in the blanks.

frames (Moores, 1967) show that deaf students have great difficulty with these tasks.

Can changes in educational procedures and/or innovative materials change these achievement levels? As reported in the Washington Post (Dec. 22, 1976), the study by the American Institute for Research on the effects of innovation on education found that second-graders given extra language skill instruction showed unusually large reading gains that year and the following one, and it suggested giving more attention to this approach. It is significant that instruction on language skills in the early educational experiences of a student seems to have positive and lasting effects upon that student's ability to cope with the routine requirements of learning within school programs.

If it is important for children with normal development to have early and intensive programs designed to develop basic language skills, it is equally important for hearing-impaired children to have such programs. Early educational opportunities must be provided hearing-impaired learners to encourage them to develop language skills which use the common symbols of their society. Hearing-impaired children are highly dependent on vision to provide most of the information for receptive communication. Sherrick (1974) described the use of one sensory system to handle the function of another system as metastatic techniques. Sensory substitutions may mean that hearing-impaired learners will have difficulty in achieving certain aspects of language skills. Although this does not mean they are not capable of developing comprehensive language skills, it does mean language development may be different for them and may require different educational techniques. These techniques should incorporate effective visual systems augmented by appropriate auditory input.

Impact of Television on Language Development

The normally hearing child is bathed in an ocean of word experiences. Word experiences are defined as either hearing or speaking a word. Each year the normally hearing child has approximately 15,000,000 word experiences. If these estimates are correct, a child entering kindergarten will have had between 75,000,000 and 80,000,000 word experiences. These word experiences will vary in richness, complexity, and style depending upon the child's family and environment.

The age of mass communication has brought about a new era of word saturation. Each television station that broadcasts for 20 hours per day creates approximately 120,000 to 150,000 word experiences daily. "Sesame Street" and other children's television programs broadcast at the rate of about 5,000 words per hour. These word experiences differ from those experiences by young children in past generations in that they are primarily passive. The average preschool child watches approximately 35 hours of television each week, which means that he or she has 175,000 passive word experiences weekly and 63,875,000 televised word experiences each year.

More than 99% of all families in the United States have at least one television set. The fact of ownership means that the television set will be used, and the average set is turned on about 6½ hours each day. Children watch the television set because it is there and requires no special skills such as reading to use it. Bernstein (1976) reported that Down Syndrome children watching "Sesame Street" attend to and learn cognitive and social skills from programs designed to model behavior.

Ambrosino (1975) explored the effect of television on self-concepts in children. She reviewed the works of Schramm, Lyle, and Parker (1961) and the Surgeon General's report (1972) on the impact of televised violence and found that:

> The content of television is increasingly a source of language, information, and socialization for the young. From the material on set, children see and imitate examples of pro- and anti-social behavior. And the more limited the child's "real" life experiences or his economic circumstances, the more likely he is to trust what he sees on the television screen. Greenberg (1972) and others have consistently found poor children and adults believing television far more than others. (p. 16)

It is reasonable to assume that handicapped children are likely to have a limited "real" life experience which makes them more susceptible to the impact of television. They may use television as a vicarious experience to expand their "real" world and to compensate for their sensory loss. Television has a unique ability to manipulate time and space. As a learning experience, television can provide relations that can be used to enhance memory, to stop action, and to associate language forms with events. Such common techniques as instant replay and stop action frames all act to expand memory. Liebergott and Swope (1976) reported on this aspect of television:

> The media have available unique characteristics for handling distancing between the child and the symbolic experience. An example of this is a segment from Sesame Street where a ball moves from a group of balls and is eaten by a fish. Initially, the fish is not a real fish, but two curved lines which touch in the beginning and cross at the end. After the ball is eaten by the fish, the camera moves in for a close-up on the curved lines. At this point, a real fish appears within the lines, and the camera moves back to reveal a group of fish swimming. For younger children, the appearance of the real fish may have narrowed the distance between themselves and the entire symbolic scene, so that they could not interpret the sequence. (p. 74)

This ability to interpose reality and symbolism has long been an asset of media formats and television techniques have expanded this ability to a practical level. It can safely be said that children watch television whether or not they fully understand the information available on the screen. Sendelbaugh (1978) indicated that hearing-impaired teenagers spend between 30 and 35 hours a week watching television even though the audio information is not fully available to them and the bits and pieces they do get may mislead or frustrate them.

In 1958 Congress passed Public Law 85-905 establishing the Captioned Films for the Deaf program designed to provide deaf individuals with the written representation of the spoken language of the film soundtrack. As television became more and more pervasive in our daily lives, this authority was expanded to include television programs (see Chapters 1 and 3). Most of the captions for both films and television are intended for the adult viewer or for the older student. Only a limited number of broadcast captions are designed for the young hearing-impaired viewer.

The interest that hearing-impaired children exhibit for television can be captured for educational purposes. Programming can be developed to provide language experiences that assist in achieving mastery of English syntax and semantics. One related effort is the Multilevel Captioning Project at The Caption Center, WGBH-TV in Boston. In a report on the project, Shulman & Decker (1979) said:

> The multi-level system is a set of guidelines for controlling the complexity of language at three reading levels . . . . It is important to note that the three captioning levels are not equivalent to the grade levels of basal readers . . . the captioned programs are a source of positive exposure to reading and will motivate hearing-impaired students to practice reading skills. Because the programs the project has chosen for captioning all contain messages of social value, they expose the deaf child to the best television offers — simple, important lessons in living, as well as basic world knowledge. (p. 560)

Technology and Learning Environments

How can technology be used more effectively to facilitate English language acquisition? Do hearing-impaired children need to be functional English language users before they begin reading instruction, or can educators assist students to master standard English through reading activities?

The acquisition of good reading and writing skills requires that there be many opportunities to practice these skills. Bruner (1963) suggested that students become learners by exploring alternative ways to solve problems and that these explorations provide feedback to the student as to why his or her solution is possible or incorrect. In the classroom, immediate feedback by the teacher is not always possible because of the many conflicting demands of the educational environment. The teacher needs assistance in providing frequent practice sessions. Writing activities are especially difficult to incorporate into classroom planning because of the need for individual attention to each child's creation. In order to provide help to the teacher in this vital area, certain criteria should be considered. Ideally, the assistance should: encourage the student to construct standard English sentences; respond to student input; provide feedback as to correctness of construction; reward the student for successful construction of the sentence; provide assistance when requested by the student; be consistent in response; be nonjudgmental; never get tired of repeating; and be easy to use and supportive of classroom activities.

For some children, intrinsic reinforcement is more effective and enduring than extrinsic rewards. Investigations into student perception of locus on control indicate that factors other than subject matter instruction influence improved achievement. For example, according to Gozali, Cleary, Walster, and Gozali (1973):

> Concern with improving achievement emphasizes instruction in subject matter. It may also be of value to teach the appropriate use of resources other than subject matter resources that are relevant to performance. (p. 10)

And in discussing reinforcement Rotter (1966) stated:

> The effect of a reinforcement . . . depends upon whether or not the person perceives a causal relationship between his own behavior and the reward. . . . The notion that individuals build up generalized expectancies for internal-external control appears to have clear implications for problems of acquisition and performance. If a human can deal with future events with the use of verbal symbols and can perceive an event as following a preceding behavior of his own, then the strength of that connection will depend at least in part on whether or not he feels there is a causal or invariable relationship between his behavior and the event. (p. 18)

Over the past 25 years technology has been increasingly employed in the education of the hearing-impaired learner. It is safe to say there is no one ideal format for all kinds of learning and teaching. Overhead transparencies, slides, films, instant still pictures and movies, captioned films, computer assisted instruction, computer-managed instruction, and television are all contributing to expanding the world of the classroom.

Computer Assisted Instruction (CAI) is being used in more and more programs and schools for the hearing impaired across the country. Von Feldt (1977) has reported a significant growth in CAI during the previous three years. Watson (1979) described a number of exciting applications of computers to instruction and communication of the hearing impaired. One of these is an interactive language instruction system for the deaf under computer control being developed by Madeline Bates of Bolt Beranek and Newman Inc. and Kirk Wilson of Boston University (Bates & Wilson, 1979). This is a microcomputer system giving the student full control over the characteristics of the tutorial language materials. The student can ask for the generation of specific language, can formulate hypotheses, and can test these hypotheses in a manner similar to the normal language learning process. This system should provide a valuable source of information about English structure and supply a significant adjunct to language acquisition in hearing-impaired children.

Another application designed to improve visual memory skills of children from kindergarten through the third grade has been developed by the Control Data Corporation working in conjunction with the Colorado Hearing and Speech Center in Denver (Watson, 1979). This CAI system uses PLATO (a large computer-based instructional system) in a drill and practice mode. These children were described as learning disabled. All had perceptual problems in the visual and auditory processing areas and some had additional speech and hearing impairments. The validation phase of the project indicated an overall increase in both visual and auditory memory skills by the children and an improvement in their learning strategies.

In a federally funded project at Gallaudet College, Withrow (1979) worked with Charles Csuri of the Computer Graphics Research Group of the Ohio State University Research Foundation to design and develop learning packages via videocassettes. The development by Csuri of three-dimensional computer graphics which can feed a videorecorder provided a unique format for associating visual and auditory images with the acquisition of language principles. This experimental technology is now at a stage of development where it is practical and cost efficient to design learning packages for use via videocassettes. The materials for this project combined animated sequences illustrating specific language principles with appropriate English language constructions. They also took advantage of the ability to present print with the language auditory signals. The entire message was shown on the screen and the message was said out loud. As the off-screen voice spoke in phrases, those phrases enlarged, indicating which phrases were being spoken at that time. This process closely associated print with audition. The outcomes of the field tests of these computer generated animated language materials were most encouraging. When all the hearing-impaired students were considered, the pretest-posttests indicated a highly significant positive improvement in student scoring. In fact, this improvement was so relevant and pervasive for the entire test application that specific differences of student samples did not show changes in this general trend.

Another recent effort to apply technology to the problems of language acquisition, reading, and writing skills integrates a microcomputer with a videotape replay system. When programmed to address specific sections of videotape, the microcomputer integrated system can find the precise portion of the videotape graphic materials in motion, color, and appropriate sound that the educator wishes to use to illustrate an instructional sequence. This is one way to expand educational environments. One such integrated system has been designed and developed at the National Technical Institute for the deaf by James von Feldt. This system affords several unusual instructional and/or research features such as: addressability of specific sections of TV tape; character generation mix during TV sequences; automatic repeat of last sequence upon student demand; upper and lower characters; unusual CAI capacities (test placement, answer analysis, data gathering, etc.); and special VTR control such as video without audio, audio without video, CAI screen control, or TV screen control.

The microcomputer integrated system is truly interactive where the student can respond to visual models related to language. When interacting with the material through the computer, the student is aware only that creating a sentence results in the action being illustrated visually on the television screen. The educator establishes the parameters of the learning sequence and the visual representation(s) of the sequence, but the student is in control of making the action appear on the screen (within the present parameters). For example, the educator may determine the number and kind of subject nouns, the types of action, and the places of action, and works within those constraints to select or develop visual sequences that illustrate all of the reasonable actions possible within those boundaries. Because the language structures can be programmed into the micro-computer as well as by controlled access to the videotape sequences, it is also possible for the educator to develop and program other appropriate language structures for the visual displays, expanding the language learning environment.

An emerging technology which may greatly alter the educational environments for both handicapped and nonhandicapped populations is that of optical videodisc. The optical videodisc is versatile, it can present visual materials in motion with two-channel audio, slow motion forward and reverse, and can find at random any one of 54,000 individual frames. This random access capability permits exciting programming for educational purposes where the student can locate specific learning sequences. Dynamic educational systems can be provided when the versatility of the videodisc is combined with the power of the computer. Galbraith, Lennan, and Peterson (1979) described a method of control of the videodisc by a small external microcomputer for use by hearing-impaired children. In addition, they modified the standard computer circuitry to supply captioning to the videodisc material. The computer floppy disc can be used to store several levels of text difficulty and the learner can select the desired level of captioning merely by typing a code into the computer keyboard.

A less sophisticated but effective method is to use these two technologies side-by-side (i.e., not physically integrated). The microcomputer is used for dialog and directs the student to specific frames of the videodisc. The student views the section of visual material on the videodisc, stops as directed, then returns to dialog with the microcomputer. In effect, the student acts as the interface between the microcomputer and the videodisc.

The U.S. Department of Education (ED) is currently engaged in a demonstration of this technique in the Washington, D.C. metropolitan area. Results of the demonstration will be shared with the field upon its completion.

It is apparent that, while hardware systems are available to enhance the educational environment for hearing-impaired learners, educational materials or software are in limited supply. If the promises of these systems are to be fulfilled, educators of the hearing impaired must become familiar with these technologies and develop learning materials appropriate to the multiple needs of the learners.

Students with Technology

In order to survive in a technology-rich society, students must learn not only to learn through technology, but also to learn to use it effectively. Shayon (1972) faulted teachers of the hearing impaired because they only use media to teach, rather than teaching children how to communicate effectively through media. He suggested that the sense of personal identity is weakened when individuals merely passively receive media messages. Thus, he urged educators of hearing-impaired children to obtain inexpensive videocameras and recorders and teach the children to use the equipment and make videotapes about their views and feelings of the world. In addition, he felt that the teacher's function was to enable the child to exploit the power of dialogue offered by the new technologies.

One application of students learning to use media to communicate is Murphy's (1974) report of freshman students at St. Mary's School for the Deaf. The students produced a news report by using various kinds of audiovisual equipment (including two video cameras with audio, an 8mm camera and projector, an instamatic camera for slides, and a transparency maker) to summarize stories from daily newspapers and show their own social news. They not only learned to use these technologies, but also developed competencies in areas such as participation, cooperation, and problem solving, increased their communication skills through group interaction, and developed reading and language skills.

Conclusion

New technologies are currently available to educators of the hearing impaired to enhance the learning environment and provide learning experiences previously unavailable to their students. These new experiences may prove to achieve higher levels of learning with greatly increased time efficiency. CAI systems have demonstrated the effectiveness of tutorial learning when the student receives immediate feedback to his or her response. With the advent of microcomputer-controlled videotape and videodisc capabilities and with real-time computer interaction, greater flexibility is available for visual display. Coordinating, organizing, and integrating these technologies to achieve desired learning goals presents an exciting challenge to educators today.

REFERENCES

AMBROSINO, L. Children's self-concepts, television and government policies. In K.W. Mielke, B.G. Cole, & R.C. Johnson (Eds.), *The federal role in children's television.* Bloomington: Institute for Communication Research, Indiana University, 1975.

BATES, M., & WILSON, K. A generative computer system to teach language to the deaf. *Proceedings of the Association for Development of Computer Based Instructional Systems,* 1979, *2.*

BERNSTEIN, L. The viewing of Sesame Street by mentally retarded children. *Children's Television Workshop,* Draft Report, 1976.

BLOOM, L. Talking, understanding and thinking. In R.L. Schiefelbusch & LL. Lloyd (Eds.), *Language perspectives – Acquisition, retardation and intervention.* Baltimore: University Park Press, 1974.

BRUNER, J.S. Needed: A theory of Instruction. *Educational Leadership,* May 1963, pp. 523-532.

CHOMSKY, N. Review of B.F. Skinner. *Verbal Behavior and Language,* 1959, *35,* 26-58.

CHOMSKY, N. *Aspects of the theory of syntax.* Cambridge, MA: MIT Press, 1965.

CLARK, E.V. Some aspects of the conceptual basis for first language acquisition. In R.L. Schiefelbusch & LL. Lloyd (Eds.), *Language perspectives – Acquisition, retardation and intervention.* Baltimore: University Park Press, 1974.

DALE, P.S. *Language development, structure and function.* Hinsdale, IL: Dryden Press, 1972.

FURTH, H.G. *Deafness and learning: A psychological approach.* Belmont, CA: Wadsworth, 1973.

GALBRAITH, G., LENNAN, R., & PETERSON, B. Interfacing an inexpensive home computer to the videodisc: Educational applications for the hearing impaired. *American Annals of the Deaf,* 1979, *124*(5), 536-541.

GOZALI, H., CLEARY, A., WALSTER, G.W., & GOZALI, J. Relationship between the internal-external control constant and achievement: Rotter's scale. *Journal of Educational Psychology,* 1973, *64,* 9-14.

LIEBERGOTT, J., & SWOPE, S. Speech and language disabilities. In F.B. Withrow & C.J. Nygren (Eds.), *Language, materials, and curriculum management for the handicapped learner.* Columbus, OH: Charles E. Merrill, 1976.

McNEILL, D. *The acquisition of language.* New York: Harper & Row, 1970.

MOORES, D. *Applications of "cloze" procedures to the assessment of psycholinguistic abilities of the deaf.* Unpublished doctoral dissertation, University of Illinois, 1967.

MURPHY, L.C. Videotape as motivator for non-hearing students, or say can you see yourself on TV and still be bored in school. *Teaching Exceptional Children,* 1974, *7*(1), 10-14.

NYGREN, C.J. Language development. In F.B. Withrow & C.J. Nygren (Eds.), *Language, materials, and curriculum management for the handicapped learner.* Columbus, OH: Charles E. Merrill, 1976.

ROTTER, J.B. Generalized expectancies for internal versus external control of reinforcement. *Psychological Monographs,* 1966, *80,* Whole No. 609.

SCHRAMM, W., LYLE, J., & PARKER, E. *Television in the lives of our children.* Stanford, CA: Stanford University Press, 1961.

SENDELBAUGH, J.W. Television viewing habits of hearing impaired teenagers in the Chicago metropolitan area. *American Annals of the Deaf,* 1978, *123*(5), 536-541.

SHAYON, R.L. Passivity versus participation: The challenge of the mass media. *American Annals of the Deaf,* 1972, *117*(5), 485-492.

SHERRICK, C.E. Sensory processes. In J.A. Swets & L.L. Elliott (Eds.), *Psychology and the handicapped child.* Washington, DC: U.S. Government Printing Office, 1974.

SHULMAN, J., & DECKER, N. Multi-level captioning: A system for preparing reading materials for the hearing impaired. *American Annals of the Deaf,* 1979, *124*(5), 559-567.

SINCLAIR-DEZWART, H. *Acquisition du langage et développement de la pensée; Sous-systémes linguistiques et opérations concrétes.* Paris: Dunod, 1967.

SLOBIN, D.I. Cognitive prerequisites for the development of grammar. In C.A. Gerguson & D.I. Slobin (Eds.), *Study of child language development.* New York: Holt, Rinehart, & Winston, 1973.

Surgeon General's Report. *Television and growing up: The impact of televised violence.* Washington, DC: United States Public Health Service, 1972.

VON FELDT, J. A national survey of CAI uses with the deaf. *Proceedings of the American Association of Computer Based Instructional Systems,* February 1977.

WATSON, P. The utilization of the computer with the hearing impaired and the handicapped. *American Annals of the Deaf,* 1979, *124*(5), 670-679.

WITHROW, M. Illustrating language through computer generated animation. *American Annals of the Deaf,* 1979, *124*(5), 549-552.

Videodisc for the Hearing Impaired

George Propp, Gwen Nugent, Casey Stone, and Ron Nugent

7

W ith the current emphasis on enriching the educational opportunities for the handicapped, it would seem that one of the top priorities would be a full-scale attack on a hearing-impaired child's mastery of the English language. A major strategy of this massive attack would be the development and application of modern communication technology. For hearing-impaired youngsters, technology might possibly provide the verbal input upon which they can base a linguistic structure, thus opening the doors of their learning potential.

It is ironic that the technology to be applied to the learning problems of the hearing impaired is one that intensified the barriers separating them from society. The telephone, radio, sound films, phonograph, television, and other electronic communication devices can all be cited as examples of technology that has worked against the hearing-impaired individual's communication with normally hearing people. Yet the same technical ingenuity that creates communication barriers can be used to reduce or eliminate them. For example, radio waves can transmit a printed page as readily as a voice, and telecommunications systems serve the hearing impaired as well as the hearing. The problem then is not one of invention, but of application.

As exemplified by the phenomenal growth in the use of TDDs (Telecommunication Devices for the Deaf), hearing-impaired consumers will use technical assistance when it is available. Much of the new technology has great applicability to the needs of the hearing impaired and may prove to be even more significant than the TDD. For example, Line 21 television captioning now makes it technically feasible to provide hearing-impaired viewers the same information received by the normally hearing. Computers offer a new dimension to learning for all types of hearing-impaired individuals. With such systems it is possible to access, through telephone lines, vast storehouses of information that are stored in computer systems throughout America. While much of the use will be in a game or other

Dr. Propp is the Associate Director of the Media Development Project for the Hearing Impaired at the University of Nebraska in Lincoln. Dr. Gwen Nugent is a Coordinator of Production and Mrs. Stone is an Instructional Designer at MDPHI. Mr. Ron Nugent is a producer at Nebraska Educational Television (NETV).

limited mode, the availability of this microcomputer technology opens up new sources of information to the hearing impaired. Predictions abound of information utilities that will be as prevalent as the telephone in America. A third development, videodisc, is a combination of television's visual display and computer assisted instruction. It might well be a significant factor in the reduction of communication barriers that separate the hearing impaired from normal society.

Videodisc History

In 1927 John Logie Baird, a British television pioneer, demonstrated that video signals could be stored on an ordinary phonograph record. Unfortunately, the technology of that period did not permit production of a clear picture, and Baird's research was dropped (Lachenbruch, 1974). But the dream of combining audio and video signals on a recordlike platter persisted and became a reality 23 years later through the efforts of a company formed by Telefunken and British Decca Records. TelDec, the first successful videodisc system developed, was demonstrated publicly in Berlin in 1970. Playing time on these initial discs was only 5 minutes, but both audio and video quality were high.

By 1974 videodisc development was in full swing. Although different systems had slightly different capabilities, all included the ability to play one specific part without having to play everything preceding it (random access) and the relatively cheap costs of mass reproduction and distribution. The videodisc was being called "the next step in the communications evolution" (Kreiman, 1974).

There are two major types of videodisc systems currently on the market in America. One is the laser disc system used by Magnavision, DiscoVision (DVA), Pioneer, Sony, and Thomson-CSF; the other is RCA's capacitance system. Laser disc — or optical — players utilize a laser light beam to read the disc and to provide the signal for the television set. This is an entirely new technology and, since the disc is read by a laser beam, there is no wear. The millionth time the disc is played is just the same as the first. The RCA capacitance system uses traditional record technology with a needle touching the surface of the videodisc.

The optical disc technology, while at a slightly higher cost on today's market, offers more versatility for the educator than the RCA discs. The optical disc can be accessed in seconds to any frame on the disc and held in view for as long as the learner needs it. Both systems offer greater accessibility than other video technologies. The optical disc, however, offers faster and better search capabilities for single frame presentations. There are about 20,000 optical home players in use today. There are more educational programs available on videodiscs in the optical format, many of which have closed captions. There are other systems in the developmental stages that may offer even greater flexibility and economies.

It is important to remember that the two systems on the American market today are not compatible; the RCA discs cannot be played on optical players and optical discs cannot be played on RCA players.

The educational advantage of the optical videodisc is that it allows for a wide range of audiovisual materials (i.e., filmstrips, audio tapes, motion pictures, still pictures) to be stored on a single disc. All of that material is easy to access by either the teacher or the learner. The major expense in videodisc reproduction is the initial master from which individual discs are duplicated. The discs themselves are relatively cheap so that, as the quantity increases, the prorated cost of the master decreases. The cost of a mass-produced videodisc library is inexpensive compared with film or videotape.

Examples of the experimental optical videodiscs developed for the hearing impaired are given later in this paper. These examples include still frame filmstriplike sections, captions, interactive computer program control, and the control of what will be presented by either the teacher or the student. This technology allows for the user to select when, where, what, and how AV materials will be presented at the user's own pace and level.

Optical videodisc systems can be roughly divided into two varieties: "home" players and educational/industrial (E/I) players. The home players, such as Magnavision, Pioneer, and DVA 7810, are less expensive but also have fewer capabilities. The E/I players, such as the DVA 7820, Sony, and Thomson, contain programmable microprocessors which permit user input, but they cost several times as much as the simpler models.

With the home players it is possible to encode chapter stops onto the videodisc in the form of digital signals. When the player is in the chapter stop mode it will automatically stop on these signals. In addition, it is possible with some players to encode picture stops so that the player will automatically stop on a given frame when it is in the play mode. E/I players do not respond to these encoded signals, but automatic stops can be programmed.

In order to locate specific sections of an optical videodisc or to know one's relationship to the rest of the program, each frame is encoded with an address or number which can be displayed or removed from the screen at the touch of a button. If the disc has been divided into chapters these numbers can also be encoded.

All optical players have two audio channels. They can contain the same audio and then be played together for stereo sound, if stereo speakers are attached, or each channel can contain a separate and distinct audio track. In the latter case, the disc could be used in different ways or with different audiences depending on which audio track was selected. For instance, one channel could be in English while the other was in Chinese, or one channel might contain instructions for the teacher while the other had student instructions. When a player is in any other mode than play, such as freeze frame or slow motion, the audio is automatically removed to avoid distortion.

Flexibility is the keystone of the optical videodisc system. Any type of audiovisual material, regardless of format, can be transferred to an optical videodisc and programs can intermix motion and still frames. With an internal microprocessor or computer interface, interactive and nonlinear program capabilities are added.

Videodisc in Education

From 1978 to 1980, the Media Development Project for the Hearing Impaired (MDPHI) at the University of Nebraska has been involved in the pioneer development, production, and evaluation of videodisc programs for hearing-impaired students. MDPHI is operating through a federal contract. The results of this contract have produced the experimental programs (not available for classroom use at this time) discussed below.

Discs developed through the MDPHI project have aimed to capitalize on the videodisc's versatility. The first disc used a multimedia approach in its design. Developed for junior high hearing-impaired students, it consists of a unit of instruction designed around a captioned Encyclopaedia Britannica film, "Israeli Boy: Life on a Kibbutz." This disc was basically a reformatting task and was designed to demonstrate the videodisc's capability to combine various media forms into a single format. Included are teacher guide materials, vocabulary instruction, filmstrip-type sequences, and interactive quiz sections. The teacher materials were extracted from the *Lesson Guide for Captioned Films* and provide objectives, suggested activities, etc. The vocabulary instruction uses visual support to define more difficult words in the film captions. The three filmstrips present instruction in specific areas, the geography of Israel and Jerusalem, and the political situation of the Middle East.

The teacher's guide, filmstrip, and quiz sequences are displayed one frame at a time, while the vocabulary and film are played in "real" time to provide motion. The quiz sections are designed for use in either a manual or computer-controlled mode. Students can respond on paper and check their answers from the feedback frame provided, or they can respond using the keyboard of an external microcomputer and be branched either to the next question or to remedial/review sequences should their answer be incorrect. One feature of the quiz is that some questions rely heavily on visual cues. For example, questions about the Wailing Wall use visuals to prompt recognition and understanding.

The multimedia approach used in this disc has certain instructional advantages, but it has economic benefits as well. If purchased separately, the film, filmstrips, television, and print materials would cost around $400. The price tag for a disc, however, could be considerably less. There is also the advantage of needing only one piece of equipment for program playback.

This disc was extensively field tested with junior high students and teachers at the Iowa School for the Deaf in the spring of 1979 and with computer interface at the Nebraska School for the Deaf. The results indicated that students had no difficulty in the use of the machine and that the videodisc was an effective tool for learning.

Another disc developed aims to teach receptive fingerspelling skills to normally hearing adults through a programmed instruction approach. A task analysis of the content resulted in the identification of a hierarchy or continuum, which prompted the development of approximately 150 sequential motion instructional sequences. Within each sequence a student is presented with a fingerspelled stimulus that requires a covert response. His or her response is then verified through feedback.

The disc is divided into two parts. The first part, visual discrimination, is designed to teach the student to notice differences between word units without looking for individual letters. The student is presented with pairs of fingerspelled words and must decide if they are the same word spelled twice or different words. The second part of the disc aims to teach students how to read fingerspelled words in sentence contexts.

The material is divided into eight sections which must be located using frame numbers, a process similar to using page numbers to locate chapters in a book. Interspersed within the instructions are four quizzes which must be completed with 90% accuracy before the student can proceed to the next section. There is also a comprehensive posttest which covers all disc material.

Instructions are given on print still frames using color-coded backgrounds. Red and green backgrounds are used for directions on operating the machine; blue backgrounds provide instructions regarding the instructional sequences. The disc was field tested with favorable results.

Developing a "visual textbook" in the area of high school literature is the approach of another disc. The primary goal of the program is to provide a positive, motivational reading experience for the hearing-impaired student through a combination of pictorial and verbal stimuli. The intent is to provide a delivery system that combines the characteristics of a textbook with the characteristics of film and still pictures. The content of the instructional task was broken down into small units that are transmitted via the most appropriate symbol system.

The theme of this disc, entitled "By Yourself," is alienation and solitude. Included are a short story, "The Pedestrian" by Ray Bradbury, two short poems, and a song. Appropriate words are highlighted and included with expanded definitions in a glossary section. In each section, motion, stills, and print are used singly or in combination to achieve the best advantage. A series of auto-stops allows movement from motion into still frame sequences. The instruction is designed for individual, rather than classroom, use since individual utilization more closely simulates textbook reading.

One videodisc has been developed for the home player, with an aim to provide parents with materials that can help them foster development and learning in their deaf child. Designed as a part of a larger package of materials, this disc relies heavily on a modeling approach and shows hearing-impaired children and their parents in typical everyday situations such as sweeping the floor and doing the laundry.

Two additional discs are intended to promote thinking skills in hearing-impaired upper elementary students. The discs are interactive, with the videodisc player and computer used together to provide computer assisted instruction. Students are branched through the disc according to their pattern of responses.

In each disc a student is presented with a problem which he or she is challenged to solve. As the child works through the disc, he or she receives instruction about various problem-solving strategies, such as problem definition and evaluation of solutions. The branching networks include more than one possible solution, so two students may each reach an acceptable, but different, problem solution. The discs aim to teach a systematic approach to problem solving, one which can be generalized to other situations.

These instructional materials integrate visuals from the videodisc and print generated from an external microcomputer. Use of computer-generated print provides greater flexibility and more efficient use of disc space. Changes in working and placement of the print can easily be initiated should field testing show the need for modification.

Finally, a disc was encoded with closed captions. The disc demonstrates the potential of videodisc to carry closed captions and helps isolate technical problems involved in the encoding process. It is entitled "Basic Tumbling Skills" and is designed to help elementary students learn the fundamentals of tumbling.

Hardware Modifications

Early in the MDPHI project it became clear that programming the videodisc through the built-in remote control unit was not sufficient for complex interactive sequences. The need for an external computer control became evident. The result was an interface between the videodisc player and the TRS-80 Radio Shack microcomputer. The microcomputer provided 48K memory capacity, and designers were able to plan interactive instructional sequences with complex branching.

The second step was a video interface which allowed computer graphics to be superimposed over the videodisc display. This union of computer and videodisc graphics eliminates the need for two display screens, one for the videodisc and one for the computer. Both can now be viewed together on one screen.

REFERENCES

KREIMAN, R.T. The videodisc: The next step in the communications evolution. *SMPTE Journal,* 1974, *83,* 553-554.

LACHENBRUCH, D. The video discs are coming. *Radio-Electronics,* 1974, *45*(8), 41-44.

Computer Assisted Instruction for the Hearing Impaired 8

IIIIIIIIIIIIIIIIIIIIIIIIIIIIIIIIIIIIIIIIIIIIIIIIIIIIIIIIIIIIIIIIIIIIIIIIIIIIIIIIIIIIIIIIIIIIIIIIIIIIIIIIIIIIIIIIIIIIIIIIII

Janice E. Richardson

Thirty years ago, the first operational digital computer was utilized on a college campus. In subsequent years, colleges and universities slowly acquired computers primarily for the purpose of research and, later, for administrative use. Twenty years ago, educational institutions began to support the use of computers for instructional purposes and, in recent years, this support has increased dramatically.

Use of computer technology for instructional purposes was slow to gain acceptance in the field of education of the deaf. The technology was expensive and there was little available evidence of successful application to this population. In addition, language difficulties inherent in the majority of available drill and practice courseware effectively blocked widespread application of this technology to a hearing-impaired audience.

Von Feldt (1978b) conducted the first systematic attempt to identify applications of computer assisted instruction with deaf student populations in 1976. A survey questionnaire was designed and sent to 237 sites; 111 were returned for a response rate of 46%. Of the 50 states surveyed, 11 were identified as having computer assisted instruction (CAI) support systems in 34 schools with a total of 408 terminals. Elementary and secondary programs were the predominant users. Of special note was the indication that schools for the deaf were not time sharing between administrative and instructional uses. Twenty-eight of the 34 computer systems were dedicated solely to CAI.

Most sites reported they anticipated rapid expansion of the application of CAI technology. Benefits identified included the potential for individualized instruction, higher motivational levels, and additional teacher time committed to instructional tasks. However, the high cost of the technology was identified as a possible deterrent to the projected expansion.

Von Feldt conducted a follow-up survey in 1980. Although survey data has not yet been completely analyzed, some trends have been identified based on preliminary examination. Sixty-two sites were identified as having computer-based support systems with a total of 781 terminals.

Dr. Richardson is Coordinator of Planning, College Educational Resources, at Gallaudet College in Washington, DC.

Approximately 674,784 hours of instructional time were provided by these systems compared to approximately 348,192 hours reported in the 1976 survey. Thus, the projected growth of the application of the technology appears to have been realized.

Four basic approaches have been identified for computer assisted instruction in programs for the hearing impaired: 1) large-scale, time-shared, dedicated systems such as PLATO; 2) intermediate- to small-scale time-shared systems such as TICCIT and CCC; 3) small-scale special purpose systems such as DAVID; and 4) general purpose microcomputers such as the PET, APPLE, and TRS 80. These alternatives reflect differences in system capacity and cost. Large-scale, time-shared systems, powered by remote CPUs (central processing units), allow the user to take advantage of the full capacity of computer technology via telephone hook-up to a remote site. On the other end of the spectrum, microprocessors represent a stand-alone technology with more limited capabilities physically located on one site. Costs vary accordingly; a microprocessor may be purchased for $600 while the lease on a single PLATO terminal may reach $1,000 per month. Since it is not possible to describe each field project within the scope of this paper, only representative projects of these four approaches will be discussed.

Large-Scale, Time-shared, Dedicated Systems

Control Data Corporation has in operation the most advanced computer-based education system in the world — the PLATO system. PLATO is a complete teaching system, assisting and managing the learning process. In an individualized, self-paced, easy-to-use manner, PLATO diagnoses, drills, tests, grades, tutors, and provides a multitude of creative activities for the learner.

Kendall Demonstration Elementary School (KDES), located on the Gallaudet College campus, in Washington, DC has been involved in a collaborative research project with Control Data Corporation for 2 years. The focus of the project has been the application of PLATO technology to young, hearing-impaired students.

Early efforts with the PLATO project focused on the field testing of the Basic Skills Math lessons, a component of the Basic Skills Learning System developed by Control Data to provide an alternative method of learning for 16- to 24-year-old, functionally illiterate adults. The package utilized both the computer-managed (management of the instructional environment) and computer assisted functions of PLATO. Observations and data gathered in conjunction with this phase of the project led to the following conclusions: 1) the students could use material independently with a minimum of preteaching; 2) there were difficulties with some of the courseware due to language problems; and 3) additional research was required to determine if and how various handicaps influence success or failure in these and other computer-based educational programs.

Additional material examined in this phase of the project included the Colorado Hearing and Speech Phase II materials designed to enhance visual memory skills. Although valid assessment of this material was not possible due to the small number of students and the relatively short time at the terminal, several conclusions were drawn, based on the experience with the material: 1) students and teachers responded positively to the lesson content and format; 2) students could sign on independently after several teacher assists; and 3) students did advance in the number of items remembered (Mackall & Richardson, 1980).

Other applications explored included use of group note files and conference calls to link hearing-impaired students and encourage language generation, use of drill and practice PLATO lessons to reinforce classroom experiences, game sessions before and after school, and experiences focusing on the visualization of sentence construction input by hearing-impaired students.

Initial experiences with PLATO at Kendall have demonstrated that students can interact independently with some of the PLATO courseware. Other courseware could be modified to facilitate use by elementary-level, hearing-impaired students; still additional courseware could be developed which would be appropriate for students with language difficulties.

Based on the initial observations of student interaction with PLATO in this environment, material developed on the Gallaudet campus concerning instructional material development for the hearing impaired, and knowledge of the student population, a set of guidelines were developed to direct future design of courseware for use by deaf students.

During the 1980-81 school year, Kendall collaborated with Control Data on the design, development, and field testing of a 6- to 10-hour segment of courseware in the area of language development. This courseware was designed consistent with the proposed guidelines and field tested in an effort to validate both the guidelines and the courseware.

During the 2-year research effort at Kendall, other PLATO sites for deaf students were identified. The Carrie Busey School and the Jefferson Middle School in Champaign, Illinois each contain classes for deaf students using PLATO as an instructional support system. These projects are tied to the Computer-Based Education Research Laboratory (CERL) at the University of Illinois and focus on the use of mathematics and phonetics lesson materials. Communication ties have been established between the Kendall School faculty and students and the staff and students in Illinois. Additional communication links have been established with students at the Hawaii School for the Deaf and Blind through the PLATO system at the University of Hawaii and with the Pennsylvania School for the Deaf in Philadelphia.

The Pennsylvania School for the Deaf has 8 PLATO terminals dedicated to the exploration of the Basic Skills Math, Reading, and Language material by secondary-level students. Additional lesson exploration is being conducted to identify courseware options for use by both elementary- and secondary-level students.

The National Technical Institute for the Deaf in Rochester, New York has also been involved in PLATO-related research. By exploring existing courseware options available through CDC PLATO, an evaluation effort is being conducted focusing on both student and teacher evaluation of identified courseware. Conversion of an IBM 1130-1500 lesson was also completed in addition to two short lessons designed to test the research capabilities of the system. NTID is not exploring the development of lessons on PLATO at this time.

In general, experience with PLATO has been rewarding. Although the initial focus was on providing drill and practice and, hopefully, tutorial courseware for hearing-impaired students, it was discovered at several sites that the by-products of exposure to computer-based education may be as important a consideration as the courseware itself. The gains in student achievement appear promising; however, the gains in student self-confidence in the process of acquiring the requisite skills to manipulate the terminal are equally promising when evaluated in the context of a handicapped child. The language generation and, perhaps more importantly, the excitement surrounding this occurrence indicates some new computer applications for hearing-impaired students in the future.

Intermediate- to Small-Scale, Time-Shared Systems

The 1976 survey of computer assisted instruction in schools for the hearing impaired indicated Computer Curriculum Corporation (CCC) systems far outnumbered others. The 1980 survey indicates this number has remained relatively stable.

As a point of clarification, CCC is not a computer company per se. Computer Curriculum Corporation rents or sells a turn-key system that provides individualized instruction in math, reading, and language arts. Unlike other systems discussed, the CCC system does not permit the user to develop lessons.

The Florida School for the Deaf and Blind entered the Stanford Computer Assisted Instruction project in 1971 (Hoffmeyer, 1980). When the federal project at Stanford was terminated, it was decided to continue computer assisted instruction efforts with the Computer Curriculum Corporation. The first computer was a free-standing M-8. Eleven teletypes were utilized to communicate with the students. Since that time, an A-16 has replaced the M-8. Students utilize the math, reading, and language material available through this system. Each student in the intermediate department has a 10 to 15 minute lesson in one of the content areas on a daily basis.

The Western Pennsylvania School for the Deaf in Pittsburgh has had a CCC system since 1976. Twenty-four terminals serve 300 students in the content areas of math, reading, and language arts. Additional efforts are currently underway to explore the use of the Apple II microcomputer to teach computer literacy.

The Washington State School is in its third year of using CCC material in the areas of reading, language, and mathematics, both at the elementary and secondary level. In general, the reaction has been positive regarding the integration of the CAI programs in the ongoing instructional programs.

The National Technical Institute for the Deaf and the Model Secondary School for the Deaf (MSSD) have also been involved in research with intermediate range, dedicated CAI systems. NTID has completed research efforts with CCC materials. MSSD has also completed a project exploring the application of TICCIT (Time-Shared, Interactive, Computer-Controlled, Information Television) to a hearing-impaired student population.

Small-Scale Dedicated Systems

The DAVID system at the National Technical Institute for the Deaf is an example of the use of a small-scale dedicated system to provide CAI support for deaf students (von Feldt, 1978a). A microbased system, DAVID combines instructional television (color, audio, motion) with computer assisted instruction. Segments of televised programs are played one at a time followed by CAI interrogation, reinforcement, branching, and performance gathering.

One area of experimental research at NTID focuses on speechreading. Utilizing existing drill and practice videotapes, students are exposed to material and then interpret the content in a self-paced mode. A second area of focus in the DAVID research effort has been to explore the multilinear branching capabilities of the system in an instructional television lesson. A live job interview sequence has been applied in this context.

Research with the DAVID system has been in progress since late 1977. Components of the prototype system include: Sony color monitors, modified industrial videotape replay unit, audio amplifier, microcomputer, keyboard, disc system, and printer. It is projected the videodisc could be substituted for the videotape system given recent technological advances in the field.

Microcomputers

Research efforts focusing on the application of microcomputer technology have increased significantly in recent years due to the rising costs of providing other types of CAI support to instructional programs. With the significant reduction of costs associated with the purchase and use of microcomputers, several sites have focused efforts on the development of courseware for use on the microcomputers.

The California School for the Deaf-Berkeley (CSDB) and the Lawrence Hall of Science at the University of California-Berkeley received a federal grant in November 1978 (Arcanin, 1979). Having been previously involved in CAI since 1970 with the Stanford Computer Assisted Instruction Project and, later, a collaborative project with the Lawrence Hall of Science, the CSDB began to focus attention on providing a less expensive delivery system than was possible under a time-shared system. After exploring the options available through microcomputer technology, a decision was made to use the Apple II system with a 48-K dual disc drive. Low resolution graphics in 16 colors provided with this configuration allow lessons, games, and student programs to reside on one disc while individual data on students, software to operate programs, and a daily record of student progress reside on the other. As the Apple II is a stand-alone machine, it eliminates both telephone and port costs. The machine is portable and can be easily integrated into the classroom.

CSDB has formed a regional network of schools composed of 8 public school districts and one private school, all located within 60 miles of the San Francisco Bay Area. Approximately 300 students from grades 2 to 12 are involved in the project. Software consultation and development was initially provided by the Lawrence Hall of Science but is now provided by Computer-Advanced Ideas in Berkeley (Arcanin & Zawolkow, 1980). Teacher involvement was judged to be critical in the development of courseware. Efforts were made to involve instructional personnel in the design of stand-alone programs written to meet the general needs of students.

A second type of locally developed program is known as an authoring system. During the development of the system, teachers work closely with programmers. Once complete, the teachers can design computer drill and practice lessons. Three basic parts comprise an authoring system: 1) the author section, comparable to writing dittos or making transparencies; 2) the student presentation section, comparable to the instructional period; and 3) record-keeping and management section.

The CSDB project has attempted to demonstrate a CAI system featuring hardware which is economically feasible and a courseware development process which emphasizes teacher involvement. The regional network concept provides an avenue for the sharing of courseware.

Conclusion

During the 20-year history of computer assisted instruction, many approaches have been utilized to apply this technology to educational programs. Large time-shared systems, turn-key systems, small dedicated systems, and micro systems are examined as educators continue in their attempt to provide a valuable support tool to the instructional setting of hearing-impaired students.

During the years of research, many questions have been raised in conjunction with the application of computer assisted instruction to the educational setting. The question of whether CAI can significantly benefit hearing-impaired students appears to have been answered in the affirmative according to the data available from active projects.

Cost continues to be a major factor in providing CAI to schools for the hearing impaired. The significant drop in cost projected by the large time-shared systems has not been realized but alternative technological advances have been proposed which allow the delivery of CAI programs at a much less expensive rate. Large, time-shared systems such as PLATO are now offering programs via micro delivery to provide alternatives for users. Thus, overall, the cost factor may be a less significant consideration in the future than it has been in the past.

Design and development efforts are expensive and, due to budget constraints on personnel money, are often not feasible. Courseware developed for hearing-impaired students must therefore be widely disseminated if we are to justify high development costs; yet, the many different types of existing delivery systems hamper such efforts.

In an effort to reduce development costs and involve instructional personnel in the design of lesson material, authoring systems have been developed for use with the microcomputer systems. While a variety of support materials can be input in this manner, the full power of the technology may not be realized under this approach.

Twenty years would appear to be a significant amount of time to have devoted to the question of computer assisted instruction yet there remains vast amounts of exploration to be done. Researchers have demonstrated the positive effect CAI support can have on academic achievement and on the motivation levels of deaf students. Exploration of the communication capabilities of PLATO and associated language and typing lessons lead us to the conclusion that computer technology may also be a powerful tool to stimulate language generation among deaf students.

Much remains to be explored. Survey data and recent publications in the field indicate that institutions serving the hearing impaired remain committed to this exploration. Hopefully, the years that lie ahead will demonstrate that the results warrant our efforts.

REFERENCES

ARCANIN, J.S. *Computer assisted instruction at the California School for the Deaf – Past, present and future: An administrator's view.* Unpublished manuscript, California School for the Deaf–Berkeley, 1979.

ARCANIN, J.S., & ZAWOLKOW, G. Microcomputers in the service of students and teachers — Computer assisted instruction at the California School for the Deaf: An update. *American Annals of the Deaf,* 1980, *125*(6), 807-813.

HOFFMEYER, D.B. Computer-aided instruction at the Florida School for the Deaf and Blind. *American Annals of the Deaf,* 1980, *125*(6), 834-840.

MACKALL, P., & RICHARDSON, J. *Computer-based education for the hearing-impaired: A look toward the future.* Unpublished manuscript presented to the International Congress on Education of the Deaf, Hamburg, Germany, 1980.

VON FELDT, J.R. *A description of a prototype system at NTID which merges computer assisted instruction and instructional television.* Unpublished manuscript, National Technical Institute for the Deaf, 1978.(a)

VON FELDT, J.R. *A national survey of the use of computer assisted instruction in schools for the deaf.* Unpublished manuscript, National Technical Institute for the Deaf, 1978.(b)

Artificial Intelligence in Computer-Based Language Instruction*

Kirk Wilson and Madeline Bates

A rtificial Intelligence (AI) is a term that arouses the interest of almost everyone who encounters it. Roughly, AI involves getting computers to do things that are normally considered to require intelligence when done by human beings. With very few exceptions, computers today show very little evidence of intelligence. Some AI researchers try to use the computer as a tool to discover how human intelligence works; others try to simulate the effect without necessarily understanding the cause. In all cases, the aim is to make computers more useful. The purpose of this paper is to extrapolate from the current capabilities of instructional AI systems to what might be feasible in the next 10 to 20 years.

AI is associated in the popular media with robots, machines that talk and understand English, and systems that solve (or help humans solve) complex problems; it has the aura of the close-at-hand-but-still-unknown future. Human intelligence is complex and does not yield easily to self-inspection so that the development of AI systems has not progressed as quickly as was originally anticipated. AI is concerned with developing computational models for such processes as vision, language understanding, knowledge representation, learning, inferring, reasoning, planning, and language production. No single system can do all of these things; none can even do one of them perfectly, yet systems have been developed that are capable of exercising an impressive amount of intelligence in a limited domain. (For a general introduction to AI, see Duda, Nilsson, & Raphael, 1979; Hunt, 1975; Jackson, 1974; Raphael, 1976; Winston, 1977.)

The implications of even semi-intelligent computer technology for education are vast (Gable & Page, 1980). By and large, computers that are available for computer-aided (assisted, mediated, managed, etc.) instruction are really quite simple in terms of what they do; they tend to be

Dr. Wilson is a research associate at Boston University in Boston, Massachusetts. Dr. Bates is a computer scientist at Bolt Beranek and Newman, Inc. in Cambridge, Massachusetts.

*This research was supported by a grant from the Office of Special Education, Department of Education, Grant #G007803230.

electronic reincarnations of the programmed workbook, relying on pre-stored questions, answers, and directions for branching created by a human teacher. (Many such systems, including TICCIT, PLATO, GNOSIS, Coursewriter, and PILOT, allow teachers to author lessons for the computer. Such systems were designed to be used by relatively naive computer users and were never intended as intelligent Computer Assisted Instruction systems.) Intelligent systems must go beyond the limitations of the "programmed" approach to become more flexible and responsive to student needs. Most intelligent systems have some understanding of the material being taught (Breuker & Camstra, 1976; Brown, Burton, & Bell, 1975; Camstra, 1976), some ability to interact with and help a student at the student's level (Burton & Brown, 1978), some approximate model of the student's thought processes (Bates, Brown, & Collins, 1979; Brown & Burton, 1978; Brown et al., 1975; Brown, Burton, Hausmann, Goldstein, Huggins, & Miller, 1977), some ability to answer questions as well as ask them (Carbonell, 1971), and/or some procedures to determine appropriate teaching strategies for a variety of situations (Bates et al., 1979; Burton & Brown, 1976; Stevens & Collins, 1977).

The Potential for AI in Language Instruction

William Blake once stated, "What is now proved was once only imagin'd." This observation is particularly apt when considering the potential of AI instruction systems of the future. To provide a concise illustration of AI instructional concepts, an imagined computer-based system which has a variety of resources to enhance a student's language ability is described in the following section. Our fanciful (though not necessarily unbelievable) script centers on a 12-year-old hearing-impaired girl named Karen and a very capable AI system which stimulates and improves her understanding and use of language. A more comprehensive simulation of educational AI systems in the 1990s is presented by Licklider (1980).

In a place not so far away and in a time not too distant Karen is starting the first part of her school day at home. After breakfast she sits down at a desk in her room which contains a color video screen, a keyboard, a microcomputer, a video/audio digital disc storage device (Luehrmann, 1977; Schneider, 1977), and several other special devices such as touchpads and stereo headphones for amplifying speech and music from the microcomputer. Karen complements her work at school using the resources of her desk to gain access to information, to communicate with her teachers, and to interact with computer systems that can function as tutors or specialists on various subjects. The initial screen display is blank except for a "menu" containing the words MAIL, DEFINE, CONFERENCE, and TUTOR. Karen starts the day by checking her "MAIL."

Reading Personal Mail

Karen looks for messages which have been sent to her and stored in her computer. (A large number of national and international computer-based communications networks now exist with simple-to-highly sophisticated capabilities for sending and receiving "electronic mail" [Rude & Mooers, 1979].) She points with a light pen to the word MAIL on her screen and new message information is immediately listed:

Date	Sender	Subject
23-Nov	Sayed Abdul Wahab: Cairo, Egypt	Exploration Simulation
24-Nov	Annette Posell: Brookline, MA	Let's Talk, OK?
24-Nov	New York Times News: NY, NY	Personalized News!
24-Nov	Annette Posell: Brookline, MA	Returned homework!

With her light-pen, Karen touches the line containing the message announcement from Sayed and the screen displays his message to her. Sayed's message was transmitted from Cairo via satellite and automatically computer-translated into third grade English from Arabic. (Automatic translation services currently exist [Farr, 1980], but not for personalizing translations to specific reading levels.) The translation helps, of course, but the message still contains some English words and phrases which Karen does not exactly understand. She gets help by pointing to the word DEFINE on the screen and then to the word she wants defined. The computer replies using vocabulary and sentence structure which Karen can understand.

Karen decides not to reply immediately to Sayed's message. She then reads the first message from Annette Posell, her English teacher, telling her that Ms. Posell will be free for a video conference at 9:00 a.m. today. The message from *The New York Times* is a computer-generated personal newspaper which contains headlines and news synopses of special interest to Karen. Karen's "news profile" includes the topics MAJOR EVENTS, GYMNASTICS, NATIONAL-SPORTS, SPACE-TRAVEL, NATIONAL-DEAF-COMMUNITY, and SANTA-BARBARA-COMMUNITY. With these keywords, *The New York Times* computer compiles each evening an index and synopsis of current news on these topics and prepares it for Karen in English which she can understand. There already exist systems that can generate English from certain data bases (Appelt, 1980; Bates & Wilson, 1979; Bates & Wilson, 1980; McDonald, 1981; Schank & Colby, 1973; Wilson & Shapiro, 1976) although more work must be done to gain control over this process and over the complexity of the English produced (Shulman & Decker, 1980).

Karen decides to check her "personalized news" before she starts her school day. Selecting the message from *The New York Times*, the video screen displays a variety of topics. Karen selects a news item about a gymnastics competition held the previous evening in Pittsburgh. At the end of the item there are directions as to how Karen can have a digital video/audio copy forwarded to her via electronic mail and stored for later viewing. If Karen wants, the audio track can be matched with computer-generated sign language interpreting or real-time captioning as she watches the gymnastics event.

Video Conference

A little after 9:00 a.m. Karen directs her computer to dial Ms. Posell for a video conference. Ms. Posell, a specialist in English language instruction for deaf students, is at her office in Sebastopol, California. Through computer mail and video conferencing (Baran, 1977), Ms. Posell stays in contact with about 100 hearing-impaired students ages 11 to 13 living throughout California. Once connected for their video conference, Ms. Posell, who also happens to be deaf, and Karen communicate as they watch each other on their video screens. Ms. Posell discusses some problems Karen has in describing characters in a story Karen wrote and directs her to review the use of "that/which clauses" with "by-sentences." Ms. Posell has written and forwarded a "prescription" for a sample lesson to Karen's Language Tutor program. Later, Karen will start up the Language Tutor and it will use the prescription to provide her with an individualized lesson on the exact grammatical topics on which Ms. Posell felt Karen should work.

Language Rules Lesson

On the recommendation of Ms. Posell, Karen decides to spend some time with the Language Tutor program reviewing "that/which clauses" and "by-sentences." (English teachers would refer to these constructions as relative clauses and passivization, but the linguistic terms are not meaningful to Karen.) While Karen spends relatively little time focusing on specific grammatical topics, occasionally such review is helpful. In this case, Ms. Posell has noticed that Karen does not seem to use the passive form for emphasis (to focus the reader's attention), and, in order to do so, she must practice not only the simple passive, but also the passive in combination with other complex forms — in this case with various types of relative clauses. (The ILIAD system is an example of such an "artificially intelligent" prescription-based language tutor, capable of producing simple-to-complex sentences to demonstrate a broad range of English sentence structures [Bates & Wilson, 1979; Bates & Wilson, 1980; Wilson & Bates, 1979].) Karen passes Ms. Posell's prescription on to her Language Tutor which creates a new grammar lesson for Karen clarifying the interaction of certain grammatical rules and exercising Karen's understanding of them.

The following dialogue illustrates Karen's interaction with the computerized Language Tutor (text created by Karen appears in italics):

> Ms. Posell suggested you study by-sentences and that/which clauses.
> You can (1) decide whether certain sentences are good or bad, (2) test your comprehension, or (3) make new sentences.
> What'll it be?
> *3*
> Here are two sentences.
>> The gorilla swallowed the banana splits.
>> I bought the banana splits.
> Write a sentence emphasizing the banana splits.
>> *The gorillas swallowed the banana splits*
>> *that I bought them.*
> Not so bad. But then again not so good either. Can I make a suggestion?
> *sure*
> Think first about "the banana splits."
> Put those words in front and then make the rest of the BY-SENTENCE. Here is an example:
> Mary painted my bike. = > My bike was painted by Mary.
> Now you try it with the following sentence:
>> Uncle Bill is fooling the girl.
>> *The girl is being fooled by Uncle Bill.*
> OK. So far so good. Now put these two sentences together and emphasize "the aunt."
>> Uncle Bill is fooling my aunt.
>> My aunt hates jokes.
>> *My aunt is being fooled by Uncle Bill who hates jokes.*
>> That's close, but no cigar!
> This is another way to think about the "that/which clause":
> My aunt
>> (my aunt hates jokes)
> is being fooled by Uncle Bill.
> Notice your error?
> *yeah.*
> OK. Now try it again.
> *My aunt who hates joks is being fooled by Uncle Bill.*
> [joks = jokes] (Here the computer spelling corrector indicates that the spelling of "joks" has been automatically corrected.)
> Outasight! Let's keep working on these.

In the above example the Language Tutor program was building a model of the language structures which Karen writes, including both grammatical and ungrammatical forms. The examples which the Tutor creates allow for a broad assessment of what Karen knows about the two main grammatical rules and the cases in which Karen does not understand their interaction. The system generates a summary report of the kinds of structures which still cause difficulties for Karen and forwards this report to her English teacher.

Although the sample dialogue emphasized topics in written language, the Language Tutor would also take advantage of amplification which produces each sentence simultaneously in a synthesized speech specifically "tuned" to Karen's speech perception and residual hearing within the speech frequencies. Similarly, the Language Tutor could provide simultaneous computer animation of manually-coded English if this were helpful to Karen in understanding the structure of sentences produced as part of the language tutorial. An alternative might also be to have American Sign Language interpretations of the practice sentences to contrast them with functionally equivalent English structures. (Proper animation of American Sign Language is an extremely difficult problem requiring sophisticated linguistic and graphics programming skills, yet some initial efforts have been made in this area [Hoemann, Florian, & Hoemann, 1976; Weyer, 1973].)

Writing Lesson

Karen then decides to work on a Social Studies/Language assignment. Mr. Ingria, her Social Studies teacher, wanted Karen to describe one of the cities visited by Marco Polo.

Karen starts her assignment by interacting with a Research Tutor program which asks Karen a number of questions about the topic to be investigated. After she indicates her topic of interest is Tashkent and its cultural geography in the 15th century, the Research Tutor displays information from a number of data bases including historical descriptions, first person accounts of Tashkent, and video images of maps, drawings, and paintings from that period. After reviewing this material, Karen creates a draft of her paper using her computer text editor. She then requests the Spelling Corrector program to check her draft for any misspellings. The Spelling Corrector corrects some words automatically (since they are in a file of Karen's commonly misspelled words), reports words that appear to be misspelled, and lists "guesses" of correct spellings for the word(s) which Karen may have intended. The program also records the misspelled words in a separate file for Karen to practice later if she is interested. (Spelling correction programs currently exist and are in wide use today; the spelling in this paper was checked by such a program. Such programs take into account likely typing errors, punctuation, prefixes and suffixes, and idiosyncratic misspellings and personal vocabularies, e.g., proper nouns. Peterson [1980] provides an excellent review of various approaches taken in designing spelling correction programs.)

With her spelling corrected, Karen directs the Grammar Tutor program to check each sentence in her draft and point out any ungrammatical expressions. The Grammar Tutor does so, paying particular attention to the that/which and by-sentences which Karen has attempted. The computer directs Karen's attention to sentences that are clearly ungrammatical, and in some cases even suggests possible corrections (Newcombe, 1975;

Weischedel & Black, 1980; Weischedel, Voge, & James, 1978). In other cases, the Grammar Tutor identifies what appears to be semantically questionable usage (such as use of pronouns where the reference is not easy to interpret). The following exemplifies how the Grammar Tutor would interact with the student:

You wrote . . .
MARCO POLO WAS PASSED A TRADER THAT LEFT TASHKENT.
This sentence has an error! Did you mean . . .
   1. Marco Polo passed a trader that left Tashkent.
   or
   2. A trader that left Tashkent passed Marco Polo.

Then you could write . . .
Marco Polo was passed *BY* a trader that left Tashkent.

You wrote . . .
HE SMILED AND WAVED HELLO.
This sentence is not clear! Did you mean . . .
   1. Marco Polo smiled and waved hello.
   or
   2. The trader smiled and waved hello.

Karen then gives the draft to a Style Tutor program (Cherry, 1981; Miller, Heidorn, & Jensen, 1981) which points out redundant sentences and overuse of certain words. The Style Tutor also suggests alternate vocabulary and idioms which Karen may use to modify her draft if she chooses. Finally, Karen processes the draft file with a text formatter (Reid & Walker, 1979) which creates a finished copy with bold-faced title, section headings, page numbering, insertion of figures from video images and Karen's hand-drawn images using a graphics tablet, and a reference list. The following example shows how the Style Tutor would prompt Karen with suggestions for improvements:

Here are 3 short sentences from paragraph 3.
You might want to combine them.
   TASHKENT WAS DIRTY.
   IT WAS VERY BIG.
   MANY PEOPLE LIVED IN TASHKENT.

In paragraph 4, you use the word TRAVELER 6 times.
Here are some other words you might want to use:
   JOURNEYER, ADVENTURER, EXPLORER, PIONEER, WANDERER,
   VAGABOND, NOMAD, WALKER, RIDER, HORSEMAN, DRIVER,
   PERSON, FELLOW, LADY, and so on.
[See 128 additional words for TRAVELER in the Thesaurus!]

Karen then forwards her draft to both Mr. Ingria and Ms. Posell who use computer text editors to insert their comments directly into the draft before it is returned to Karen the same day. When Karen receives the edited drafts she makes revisions and then resubmits her draft to her teachers.

Language and Inference Comprehension

Moving to another school subject, geography, Karen learns about weather patterns as well as something about how to infer from available information. (The following computer-student dialogue is a real, though edited and annotated, example of how a student conducts a dialogue with the WHY system [Bates et al., 1979] developed at Bolt Beranek and Newman. Text following the symbol *** was typed by the user; all other text was typed by the computer.)

We will be discussing why rainfall occurs in Ireland. Ireland has fairly heavy rainfall. In order to have heavy rainfall there must be a lot of moisture in the air. For Ireland the moist air comes from over the Gulf Stream Current. How does moisture get into the air over the Gulf Stream?
***It evaporates from the Gulf Stream.
Why does a large amount of moisture in the Gulf Stream evaporate into the air mass over the Gulf Stream?
***Because the air is warm.
Yes, what else makes it possible for a large amount of moisture to evaporate?
***I don't know.
Because the water in the Gulf Stream is warm, a large amount of water can evaporate into the air mass over the Gulf Stream. What happens after the air mass absorbs a large amount of moisture from the Gulf Stream?
***The moist air is blown to Ireland by the wind.
Right. What happens after the air mass over the Gulf Stream moves to over Ireland?
***The moisture condenses.
That is true, but you left some things out. Why does the moisture in the air mass over Ireland condense?
***It cools.
Correct, what else makes it possible for condensation to occur?
***The air is moist.
Yes. What happens before the moisture in the air mass over Ireland condenses?
***It rises.
That is true but you left some things out. Why does the air mass from over the Gulf Stream rise over Ireland?
***It must be cooled.
Well that is involved in causing rainfall, but it happens later in the process. Because the air mass from over the Gulf Stream is warmer than the air mass over Ireland it can rise. What happens when the air mass from over the Gulf Stream rises over Ireland?
***Now it cools.

Correct, what happens after the air mass over Ireland cools?
***The moisture condenses.
Right, what happens to the moisture in the air mass when that moisture condenses?
***It falls as rain.
Yes, and what happens to the humidity of the air mass over Ireland after the moisture in it condenses?
***The humidity becomes lower.
Yes, that's right. That is all for now.

In this example one can see that the computer can "understand" very natural English typed input, and responds appropriately to the user in all cases. In addition, the system attempts to lead the user toward a particular model of weather processes, recognizes when the user has said something right but not exactly relevant to the current question (the "but you left something out" responses), and determines the content of each question based partly upon the user's answer to the last question.

Speech Lesson

Karen must complete a speech lesson each day since together with her speech teacher, Gunnar Kahrstrom, she has set a 3-month target for a certain level of intelligibility and proper intonation.

The Speech Tutor program is similar to the Grammar Tutor in that it uses prescriptions provided by Ms. Kahrstrom who meets with Karen three times a week for speech therapy. For today's lesson Karen will be concentrating on intonation in complex sentences. The Speech Tutor starts by asking her whether she has done any writing lately which could be used as part of the sentence intonation lesson. Karen indicates that both her Marco Polo essay and her session with the Grammar Tutor contain complex sentences. The Speech Tutor displays one of the sentences from the Marco Polo essay and "speaks" it using synthetic speech. As the sentence is spoken, a small, animated image of a girl hops across each word, syllable by syllable, showing Karen the proper pacing and the intensity with which each syllable is spoken. Karen is then given an opportunity to practice her intonation on this sentence with the same animated girl moving correctly or incorrectly across each word Karen pronounces. Karen may have the correct intonation pattern animated at the same time as an animation sequence displays her own speech; she compares her speech pattern with that of the computer's idealized model by observing similarities between the two animation sequences. Although the lesson does not focus directly on articulation, Karen may request that the basic articulation form of a word be displayed in a simplified phonetic form (e.g., phone = FOAN). Nickerson and others have investigated a variety of such computer-based approaches to speech instruction for deaf students (Boothroyd, Archambault, Adams, & Storm, 1972; Nickerson, 1975, 1979; Nickerson,

Kalikow, & Stevens, 1976; Nickerson & Stevens, 1972, 1976a, 1976b, 1977; Nickerson, Stevens, Rollins, & Zue, 1979).

Following her more formal speech lessons, Karen takes a break by playing her favorite computer game, Monster Hunt. To play this game, she must give spoken commands. Low-cost systems, such as the Heuristics speech understanding system and Cognivox, currently exist and can be bought "off the shelf" to recognize a limited vocabulary of spoken words and phrases. The recognition of natural, connected speech has also been accomplished by some research systems, with considerable restrictions on vocabulary and grammar (Dixon, 1977; Klatt, 1977). The computer in the beginning of the Monster Hunt game accepted (i.e., "understood") rather unintelligible speech, but Karen's teacher has, over a period of weeks, tightened the speech understanding parameters so that Karen's articulation must be more accurate for her commands to be understood. Thus, without her being aware of it, the games serve as a subtle and effective motivation for Karen to improve the intelligibility of her speech.

The Future of AI in Language Instruction

The scenarios we have presented here are not science fiction — each one is well within the potential of AI in the next few years. One of the problems we now face is anticipating the course of development that these computer technologies will take. It is clear that personal computers within the next decade will be at least as powerful as large computers are today (Braun, 1977), and that tying into networks of computer systems will provide low-cost capabilities far in excess of what is already available. These computers will give an individual access to an unimaginable amount of information through data bases stored throughout the world and accessed by satellite communications.

But access to a lot of data does not ensure an education. In order to take advantage of this resource, computers must be able to process the information they store in more than a passive way. They must be able to understand their data (at least to some extent) and to communicate about it to their computer users in the way that is most natural for people to understand, using English, French, Chinese, and so on. As we build computer systems more adept at producing and understanding language, we will have the tools to build systems to teach about language as well. Thus, what some people now consider "pure AI research" is actually very close to the applied development of AI systems for education.

The immediate goal of AI in education will not necessarily be to implement systems like those described above or other applications of AI for diagnosing language ability, managing instruction (prescribing language learning activities), building vocabulary, improving listening comprehension skills, developing reading skills, or teaching higher level skills (rhetoric, poetry, etc.). More important will be the ability of this discipline to arrive at some general principles for instruction via AI tutorials. Some basic operating principles would include the following: 1) tutorials must be intrinsically motivating; 2) tutorials should be highly entertaining, allowing voice commands and adaptive speech understanding and graphic display interfaces; 3) language should be learned in functional contexts and didactic approaches should be used at the student's request (i.e., the student should assume responsibility for language learning); 4) tutorials should be sensitive to the student's level of language understanding so that computer-generated directions, advice, questions, and so on are easily understood; and 5) diagnostic and assessment information should be made available to students and teachers in a useful form.

It is important to note that in these idealized scenarios we have not eliminated human teachers, but rather have envisioned a set of tools that augment the efforts of a human teacher and present an environment in which the student can practice and master the skills and concepts taught by that teacher. The increased language exposure of "electronic mail" and the individualized dialogues and diagnoses of "intelligent" tutors will provide teachers with a greater range of resources with which to help students acquire both the simple and the highly complex aspects of language use.

In addition to a consensus on the goals of AI in instruction, a number of additional prerequisites will need to be met before the promise of AI in instruction is fulfilled. Computer hardware will need to drop further in price. Software will have to become more sophisticated to provide AI researchers with the tools to enable development of sophisticated systems. And, AI itself will advance as psychologists, linguists, and educational researchers better understand their respective disciplines and help to integrate their knowledge into AI implementations. Since AI in instruction implies a cross-disciplinary effort, it will require a critical mass community with useful communication among educators, researchers in educational technology, and scientists developing AI systems. The final two prerequisites are the most important. In order of importance, they are 1) teachers and students must lend their moral support to those who are testing new ideas and systems for AI instruction, and 2) financial support for AI research in instruction, despite the relatively high initial costs.

REFERENCES

APPELT, D.E. Problem solving applied to language generation. *Proceedings of the 18th Annual ACL Meeting*, June 1980.

BARAN, P. Interactive two-way communications via TV cable to the home for educational purposes — Why is nothing happening? In *Computers and communication: Implications for education*. New York: Academic Press, 1977.

BATES, M., BROWN, G., & COLLINS, A. *Socratic teaching of causal knowledge and reasoning*. San Diego: Conference of the Association for the Development of Computer-Based Instructional Systems, February, 1979. (Bolt Beranek and Newman Rep. 3995, 1978)

BATES, M., & WILSON, K. *A natural language micro-computer system for English instruction*. Washington, DC: Society for Learning Technology, 1979.

BATES, M., & WILSON, K. *Artificial intelligence in microcomputer-based systems*. Vancouver, BC: Instructional Technology, 1980.

BOOTHROYD, A., ARCHAMBAULT, P., ADAMS, R., & STORM, R. *Use of a computer-based system of speech training aids for deaf persons*. Washington, DC: A.G. Bell Assn. for the Deaf, 1972.

BRAUN, L. A speculation of the impact of LSI technology on computing. In *Computers and communication: Implications for education*. New York: Academic Press, 1977.

BREUKER, K., & CAMSTRA, B. *Concept-based computer assisted instruction* (Tech. Rep. 7601-01). COWO, 1976.

BROWN, J.S., & BURTON, R.R. Diagnostic models for procedural bugs in mathematics. *Cognitive Science*, 1978, *2* (2), 176-204.

BROWN, J.S., BURTON, R.R., & BELL, A.G. Sophie: A step toward creating a reactive learning environment. *International Journal of Man-Machine Studies*, 1975, *7*, 675-696.

BROWN, J.S., BURTON, R.R., HAUSMANN, C., GOLDSTEIN, I., HUGGINS, B., & MILLER, M. *Aspects of a theory for automated student modelling* (Tech. Rep. 3549, ICAI Rep. No. 4). Cambridge, MA: Bolt Beranek and Newman, May 1977.

BURTON, R.R., & BROWN, J.S. A tutoring and student modeling paradigm for gaming environments. In *Symposium on Computer Science and Education*, proceedings of a Conference held in Anaheim, CA, in February 1976.

BURTON, R.R., & BROWN, J.S. An investigation of computer coaching for informal learning activities. *International Journal of Man-Machine Studies*, 1978, *11*(1), 5-24.

CAMSTRA, B. *Make CAI smarter*. Heidelberg, Germany: Second International Conference on Improving University Teaching, 1976.

CARBONELL, J.R. *Mixed-initiative man-computer instructional dialogues. Cambridge, MA: Bolt Beranek and Newman, 1971. (Tech. Rep.)*

CHERRY, L.L. Writing tools — The STYLE Diction Programs, *Computing Science* (Tech. Rep. No. 91), February 1981, Bell Laboratories.

DIXON, N. Automatic recognition of continuous speech: Status and possibilities for an operational system. In *Computers and communication: Implications for education*. New York: Academic Press, 1977.

DUDA, R.O., NILSSON, N.J., & RAPHAEL, B. State of technology in artificial intelligence. In P. Wegner (Ed.), *Technical note 211: SRI international*. Cambridge, MA: MIT Press, 1979.

FARR, R. *Weidner computer-assisted translation system*. Provo, UT: Weidner Communications, Inc., 1980. (Tech. Documentation)

GABLE, A., & PAGE, C.V. The use of artificial intelligence techniques in computer-assisted instruction: An overview. *International Journal of Man-Machine Studies*, 1980, *12*, 259-282.

HOEMANN, H., FLORIAN, V., & HOEMANN, S. *A computerized model of the structure of deaf sign language*. Unpublished paper, 1976.

HUNT, E.B. *Artificial intelligence*. New York: Academic Press, 1975.

JACKSON, P.C. *Introduction to artificial intelligence*. New York: Petrocelli Books, 1974.

KLATT, D. Review of the ARPA speech understanding project. *Journal of the Acoustical Society of America*, 1977, *62*(6), 1345-1366.

LICKLIDER, J.C.R. Social and economic impacts of information technology on education. (Paper presented at the Joint hearings of the Subcommittee on Science, Research, and Technology, April 2-3, 1980, 96th Congress.) Government Printing Office reprint #67-283 O, pp. 76-113.

LUEHRMANN, A. Intelligent video disc systems — Implications for education. In *Computers and communication: Implications for education*. New York: Academic Press, 1977.

McDONALD, D. *Natural language production as a process of decision-making under constraint*. Ph.D. thesis, Massachusetts Institute of Technology, 1981.

MILLER, L., HEIDORN, G., & JENSEN, K. Text-critiquing with the EPISTLE system. Paper presented at the May 1981 National Computer Conference in Chicago, IL.

NEWCOMBE, W. *Status report: The development of a computer based language instruction system for teaching English at the National Technical Institute for the Deaf*. Rochester, NY: Center for Communications Research, 1975. (Tech. Rep.)

NICKERSON, R. *Speech training and speech reception aids for the deaf* (Tech. Rep. 2980). Cambridge, MA: Bolt Beranek and Newman, 1975.

NICKERSON, R. *Research on computer based speech diagnosis and speech training aids for the deaf* (Tech. Rep. G00-76-0116). Cambridge, MA: Bolt Beranek and Newman, 1979.

NICKERSON, R., KALIKOW, D., & STEVENS, K. Computer-aided speech training for the deaf. *Journal of Speech and Hearing Disorders*, 1976, *41*(1), 120-132.

NICKERSON, R., & STEVENS, K. *An experimental computer-based system of speech training aids for the deaf*. Cambridge, MA: Institute of Electrical and Electronics Engineers and Air Force, Cambridge Research Laboratories, 1972.

NICKERSON, R., & STEVENS, K. *Speech training aids for the hearing impaired*. Washington, DC: Society for Applied Learning Technology, 1976. (a)

NICKERSON, R., & STEVENS, K. Using a computer to help teach deaf children to speak. In *Science, Technology, and the Handicapped*. Washington, DC: American Association for the Advancement of Science, 1976. (b)

NICKERSON, R., & STEVENS, K. Implications for the hearing-impaired of computer-related research in human communication. *Journal of the Acoustical Society of America*, 1977, *62*(Suppl. 1, S91).

NICKERSON, R., STEVENS, K., ROLLINS, A., & ZUE, V. Computers and speech aids. *Proceedings for the Conference on Speech of the Hearing Impaired: Research, Training, and Personnel Preparation*, Oct. 31, Nov. 1 & 2, 1979.

PETERSON, J.L. Computer programs for detecting and correcting spelling errors. *Communications of the American Computing Machinery*, 1980, (12), 676-687.

RAPHAEL, B. *The thinking computer*. San Francisco: W.H. Freeman and Co., 1976.

REID, B.K., & WALKER, J.H. *Scribe User's Manual*. Pittsburgh, PA: UNILOGIC, Ltd., 1979.

RUDE, R.V., & MOOERS, C.D. *Hermes message system: Reference manual*. Cambridge, MA: Bolt Beranek and Newman, 1979.

SCHANK, R., & COLBY, K. (Eds.). *Computer models of thought and language*. San Francisco: W.H. Freeman and Co., 1973.

SCHNEIDER, R. Applications of videodisc technology to individualized instruction. In *Computers and communication: Implications for education*. New York: Academic Press, 1977.

SHULMAN, J., & DECKER, N. *Readable English for hearing-impaired students: Multi-level guidelines for linguistically controlled reading materials*. Boston: The Caption Center, WGBH-TV, 1980.

STEVENS, A., & COLLINS, A. *The goal structure of a Socratic tutor* (Tech. Rep. 3518). Cambridge, MA: Bolt Beranek and Newman, March 1977.

WEISCHEDEL, R., & BLACK, J.E. Responding intelligently to unparsable inputs. *American Journal of Computational Linguistics*, 1980, *6*(2), 97-110.

WEISCHEDEL, R., VOGE, W.M., & JAMES, M. An artificial intelligence approach to language instruction. *Artificial Intelligence*, 1978, *10*, 225-240.

WEYER, S. *Fingerspelling by computer* (Tech. Rep. 212). California: Stanford Institute for Mathematical Studies in the Social Sciences, 1973.

WILSON, K., & BATES, M. *A generative computer system to teach language*. San Diego: Assn. for Development of Computer-based Instruction System, 1979.

WILSON, K., & SHAPIRO, P. *ILIAD: Interactive language instruction aid for the deaf*. Santa Barbara, CA: Assn. for the Development of Computer-based Systems, 1976.
WINSTON, P.H. *Artificial intelligence*. Reading, MA: Addison-Wesley, 1977.

Future Implications
for Technology in the 80s

Harriet G. Kopp

10

E xamination of the preceding chapters leads to the inescapable conclusion that technological advances have surpassed our capability to use
them effectively in the education and rehabilitation of persons with impaired hearing. The technological state of the art reflects the funding of
research and production priorities of World War II and subsequent military
actions and the scientific pressures of the Cold War years. War driven
efforts to develop privacy communication systems, to improve transmission of coded and transformed speech, and to track acoustic signals
generated by equipment, human, and such nonhuman sources as plankton,
shrimp, and mosquitoes led to the interest in speech analysis and synthesis
which resulted in the production of the sound spectrograph and the real-
time visible speech display almost 40 years ago. A direct spin-off of
research in military devices and space technology was the priority given to
miniaturization, transistors, solid state circuitry, signal compression,
microchips, microprocessors, and computers. Sophisticated, high fidelity
acoustic and video recording and playback devices, including storage and
retrieval capabilities, have provided a basis for the hearing aids and
auditory testing equipment of the 80s and the video technology we take for
granted.

Although education of the handicapped received significant federal
funding during the 60s and 70s, we have not seen the hoped for, widespread
application of the new technologies to education and rehabilitation. Nor
have we attained the goals identified in three decades of federally funded
National Conferences on Deafness. While we may agree with Browning
that "a man's reach should exceed his grasp," it is instructive to explore the
issues that may be responsible for our present state and that must be
resolved if the 80s are to become a decade of fulfillment rather than
promise.

Communication Transmission Modes

It is recognized that communication is the single most significant
problem facing hearing-impaired individuals. Choice of input-output

---

Dr. Kopp is Acting Dean of the College of Human Services at San Diego State University in San Diego, California.

communication modes and competency in their use affect every aspect of an individual's life — personal-social, cultural, economic, intellectual, vocational, and psychological. The key to language acquisition is communication in its broadest sense. Unfortunately for the hearing impaired, the language used in our culture was designed primarily for acoustic transmission. The accompanying nonverbal messages, referred to as body language, are interpreted as unconscious modifiers of verbal output, either reinforcing or negating the information. Reading and writing are second order visual transmission modes not accessible equally to all civilized peoples, although considered as essential in our present culture. Such other visual transmission modes as sign language, fingerspelling, and speechreading (unaided by hearing), communicate the lingua franca of our culture with varying degrees of precision and require that both sender and receiver possess special skills.

Language Learning and Computer Assisted Instruction

Attempts to adapt technology to accelerate language acquisition sharpen our focus on a wide range of questions and assumptions. How can we provide computer assisted diagnostic and prescriptive language software in interactive instruction, employing the particular complex of audio/visual/tactile supplementation suitable for each individual at a given developmental stage? How do we select appropriate learning strategies to achieve specified cognitive processing competencies? The issue here is, in part, the organization of input information (Kopp, 1968, pp. 33-41) to permit efficient perception, differentiation, storage, and retrieval in order that output may be assessed. A simplified, cognitive processing model (see Figure 1) indicates the multiplicity of decisions requisite prior to undertaking development of a learning "package" whether it be destined for classroom, tutorial, laboratory, independent learning, diagnostic teaching, or interactive software. A few courageous researchers have produced the software referred to in previous chapters. However, evaluation has been sporadic and, in most cases, is still in process.

The availability of authoring systems and inexpensive microcomputers will lead to successful results only if those developing the basic software are competent in organizing interactive instruction and knowledgeable about language acquisition systems, cognitive processing hierarchies, and the potential range of learning strategies afforded by CAI or CMI (Computer Managed Instruction). It is inevitable that such software will be produced cost-effectively only by specialized production groups for wide-range sharing as a basis for modification by individual teachers.

An integral part of CAI or CMI programs is the ability to accumulate data on individual or group performance responses. The potential for analysis of error patterns, for decision making on selection of learning

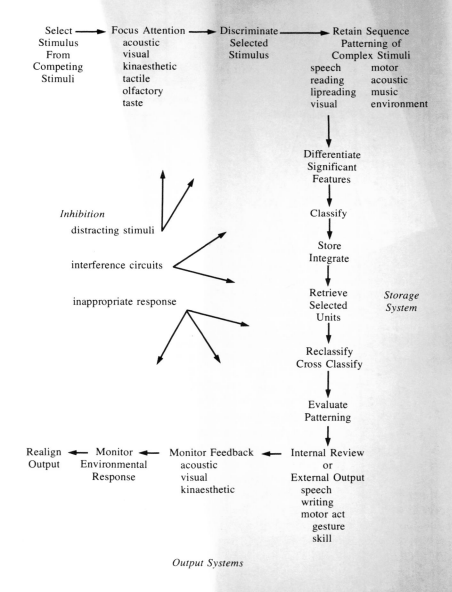

Figure 1.   Cognitive processing model (from: Kopp, H.G. Curriculum: Cognition and content. *The Volta Review*, 1968, *70*(6), 377.)

strategies/materials/modes (Kopp, 1966), and for longitudinal assessment of learning has not been realized heretofore except by a superlative teacher-diagnostician, head-on-head with a single pupil. Teacher preparation programs will be under pressure to assure that teachers understand cognition and curricular development and are skilled in diagnostic/ prescriptive strategies. The lock-step, workbook syndrome should meet a well-deserved death.

Integration of language acquisition and performance competencies with subject matter learning should raise achievement levels of hearing-impaired students and, perhaps, of their normally hearing peers (Kopp, 1979). Students who have learned to write using the editing capabilities of a networked microcomputer, experiencing such joys as electronic mail, directory assistance, and spelling correction, will demand tutorial feedback and will expect short latent period reinforcement. Success resulting from individually paced "challenge programs" will be self-motivating, encouraging independence and responsibility for learning.

Although the inherent interdependence of reading and writing are recognized, the near identity of cloze* competencies in both modes has not been exploited sufficiently by teachers in the past. CAI and CMI make it possible to assure that input and output language competency can be evaluated by the ability to manipulate language structures actively and independently and to process psycholinguistically in order to acquire and impart information (Kopp, 1980).

Hearing Aid Technology

Much social/vocational communication is directly interpersonal without intervening print, even in real-time display. Historically, debate has centered on the rationale for, and effectiveness of, oral/aural communication skills by those who are prelingually hearing impaired. If the potential for delivery of acoustic information in prespecified forms is reached in this decade, it could significantly facilitate the achievement of usable oral skills. Research must focus on areas which will make diagnostic/ prescriptive hearing aids an effective reality. The answers are not yet in on accommodation for perceptual distortion effects; relative value of enhancement of auditory asset zones or compensation for deficit zones; long-term effects of frequency transposition and band width compression; phonetic feature extraction; and true binaural versus quasi-binaural aids. The significance of the minimal essential cue (Kopp, 1943, 1978) in the intelligibility of continuous speech perception and production has been hypothesized since 1943 (Potter, Kopp, & Green, 1948), used extensively in speech synthesis and analysis, but not yet applied in hearing aid produc-

---

*The ability to derive meaning from partial information as in reading or visual perception.

tion. A different rationale for significant feature extraction may be found in presbycusis. In addition, the special auditory processing problems characteristic of the aging population have not been addressed aggressively in research, using the acquired competencies in auditory cloze processing as a basis for simplification of the input signal.

The potential for invasive implantation of electro-stimulators as aids has only been scratched. Rehabilitation engineering has made giant strides in the past decade in implantation of proprioceptive aids, prosthetic appliances, and motor stimulators. Surgical transplantation of organs leads inevitably to hope for the ultimate solution to hearing disability. Although effective binaural implants may not be achieved in this decade, the problems explored should result in solutions to the simplification of acoustic input at a level serviceable for those hearing-impaired individuals who do not find present hearing aids effective.

Research in progress in dichotic listening, voice onset time, determinants of speech intelligibility under adverse listening conditions, noise suppression, electro-cutaneous supplementation, and suprasegmental feature cues as related to speech comprehension provide a data base for experimental modification of currrent hearing aids. Computer technology may make the long-awaited master diagnostic/prescriptive hearing aid a legitimate goal.

Finally, decades of maintenance problems and the passive acceptance of fragile hearing aids by consumers, coupled with the failure of consumers, manufacturers, and concerned professionals to collect substantive performance data should provide impetus, in this decade, for collaborative efforts to reduce purchase and maintenance costs, thus making use of residual hearing more accessible. Hearing aid "down time" is a pervasive problem that interferes with continuity of auditory programs, limits user satisfaction and motivation, and increases cost over time.

Communication Output

Since oral language is normally acquired through auditory input and production competency achieved through auditory monitoring and matching by trial and error, individuals with prelingual hearing impairment are at a significant disadvantage. Acquisition of speech at a level intelligible to society at large has been difficult without aided acoustic feedback, intensive supplemental instruction, and strong familial/social support. Although a number of speech aids providing visual feedback at varying levels of complexity have been available, they have not been employed widely. The more sophisticated, real-time devices affording visual analogs of acoustic/speech output have required systematic, longitudinal instruction individually or in small groups by teachers with specialized preparation in physiologic phonetics, phonology, and speech science, as well as articulation theory and methods. In addition, these devices tend to be relatively expensive and to require frequent skilled maintenance.

Supplemental feedback devices providing visual displays of single features have been used sporadically. The advent of digital processing should, in this decade, provide high quality, real-time visual feedback, accessible in cost, but which will continue to require teachers with advanced interdisciplinary specialization in speech, audiology, phonology, and linguistics. The results of four decades of speech analysis and synthesis have led some researchers to forget that human speech is the product of an organism involving the interaction of sensorimotor systems and cognitive/linguistic processing at extraordinary rates with seemingly infinite variation and minute physiological tolerances.

Evaluation of Technology

Much of the assessment of the effectiveness of instructional intervention, teaching/learning strategies, supplemental devices, and communication modes has been based on short duration, small sample, single-controlled variable studies. Data so derived is insufficient to provide persuasive evidence of efficacy. Problems of sampling are exacerbated by the complicated variables inherent in a population of hearing-impaired individuals. It is difficult to match controls while accounting for such factors as: age; onset of hearing loss (pre/postlingual); extent, etiology, and nature of hearing loss; communication experiences and competencies; concommitant perceptual/motor or learning problems; aided threshold; home conditions; and psychosocial status.

Even longitudinal studies of reasonable sizes are problematic, since concatenating variables are altered differentially over time. The moral issues raised by withholding successful devices or instructional strategies and by experimentally applying methods of unknown value versus approved methods bring into question the use of control/experimental groups except for exceedingly short studies. The problem is particularly acute with young deaf children due to the time pressure of learning relative to readiness stages. Inability to accumulate clean, hard data appears to encourage a pernicious condition characterized by Cartailhac as "mea culpa d'un sceptique" (Broderick, 1963), preventing the rational evaluation of performance and encouraging early rejection of that which is new, different, or complex.

Communication Input

Perhaps, in the next decade, selection criteria will evolve for free choice of communication modes according to prime need and capability rather than forced choice because of accessibility, inadequacy of resources (personal, educational, medical, social, financial), and emotional bias. Input modes, such as speechreading, may be accessed more readily if wearable cueing devices can provide visual/tactile cues to such acoustic features as voice onset, plosion, nasality, and friction. Audition may be accepted more widely as a viable input mode for prelingually deaf children if individually prescribed hearing aids and integrated home/school programs are available.

Current research in children's acquisition of sign language should assist in assessing the relationship of sign to other language systems (Bellugi & Klima, 1979, pp. 99-117) and in evaluating the variant forms of sign now competing for educational application. There has been little research consideration of the bilingual problems engendered when the hearing-impaired child must learn a second language system with a different or variant input mode. Furthermore, little is known about the perception, storage, and retrieval of sign, fingerspelling, or speechreading as either sole input modes or as they interact when used conjointly. There has been no significant body of research focused on intermodality transfer associated with the simultaneous, sequential, or alternative use of various input modes: auditory, tactile, visual (sign, fingerspelling, speechreading, reading). Nor have studies focused on the differential cognitive processing loads inherent in the parameters of audition, vision, and taction, including perceptual resolution, temporal versus spatial organizations, and short- and long-term memory. Examination of data on the maturation rates of neurophysiological systems coupled with knowledge of developmental readiness stages may lead to dispassionate selection of differential criteria for the choice of a particular input mode for a given individual at a specified age.

Although reading should be the most efficient of all information input modes, it is usually the least effective for the hearing-impaired individual since it is language dependent (Kopp, 1963, 1967, pp. 1524, 1526). The potential for use of CAI and CMI in developing reading/writing competencies through psycho-linguistic processing is, perhaps, our most promising hope for the next decade.

Transformation of Acoustic Information

Isolation of hearing-impaired individuals at home may be diminished significantly if real-time captioning for television is extended and funding continued for expansion of education and recreational programming. The impact of telecommunication aids on vocational choices and mobility has been evident. However, the potential of videophones for transmission of information in multiple communication modes has not yet been realized in the workplace, the home, or the school. For example, master teachers could participate in interactive teaching using telephone lines to bring geographically and educationally isolated students into group and tutorial programs. Such technology could also provide counseling services, medical advice, and increased vocational independence to a population not served by audio amplification alone.

The advent of portable speech synthesizers, even with the limitation of controlled vocabulary and lack of immediate spontaneity, could provide intelligible speech output when a TDD (Telecommunications Device for the Deaf) network is either not available or not appropriate. For those with limited oral competence, development of inexpensive, portable, real-time speech analyzers could close the telephone communication loop when coupled with speech synthesizers. For others, they could provide a continuous feedback source for speech maintenance. Recognition of real-time spectrographic display of a controlled vocabulary of phrases and sentences has been demonstrated by congenitally deaf adults and children (Potter, Kopp, & Kopp, 1966, pp. iii-vi). The further development of the necessary technology seems to be dependent upon anticipated industrial and space applications in the next decade.

It is feasible, in this decade, to expect that alternative signals will be widely available to meet such needs of daily living as: emergency output communications (fire, police, medical); child care (crying, coughing); alarm systems (public buildings, home); and alerting systems (car, plane, door, phone, cooking appliances). The technology is available; consumer pressure is the requisite agent for marketable applications.

Funding Resources

One issue that may be revived, in this decade, is that of mainstreaming the severely hearing impaired, particularly at lower grade levels. Criteria for mainstreaming cannot be evaluated independently of the resources for tutorial supplementation, compensatory education, and supportive personnel. The distribution pattern of educational funding resources has not been assessed differentially with respect to the cost effectiveness of various delivery systems as they are applied to individuals with specified levels of hearing disability. Emphasis on small group and individualized prescriptive teaching programs oriented to specialized needs and organized around CAI laboratory/classroom networks could either facilitate or preclude mainstreaming depending upon funding patterns.

It is clear that the present limitation on funding resources and the increased competition for available financial support will intensify pressures on those who pursue research and demonstration projects. The selection of funding priorities may reflect political realities rather than issue/direction choices. The technology is available, the need pervasive. Only through the collaborative effort of industry, government, the professions, and the consumer will this decade realize its promise for the hearing impaired.

358 *Kopp*

REFERENCES

BELLUGI, U., & KLIMA, E.S. Language: Perspectives from another modality. In *Brain and Mind* (Ciba Foundation, Symposium 69), *Excerpta Medica,* 1979.

BRODERICK, A.H. *The Abbé Breuil, prehistorian.* London: Hutchinson, 1963.

KOPP, H.G. *Some functional applications of basic phonetic principles.* Ann Arbor: Edwards Letter Press, 1943.

KOPP, H.G. *Some functional applications of basic phonetic principles.* San Diego: Neyenesch Printers, 1978.

KOPP, H.G. Silent reading for the deaf. *American Annals of the Deaf, Proceedings of the International Congress on Education of the Deaf,* 1963, *108*(3), 290.

KOPP, H.G. Applications of systems concept to teaching the deaf. *American Annals of the Deaf,* 1966, *111*(5), 668-675.

KOPP, H.G. Reading as an input function. In *Proceedings of International Conference on Oral Education of the Deaf.* Washington, DC: Alexander Graham Bell Assn. for the Deaf, 1967.

KOPP, H.G. Problems of perception and cognition among the disadvantaged. In A.J. Tannenbaum (Ed.), *Special Education and Programs for Disadvantaged Children and Youth.* Reston, VA: The Council for Exceptional Children, 1968.

KOPP, H.G. Deafness and learning. *Science Education News,* 1979, Fall-Winter.

KOPP, H.G. Applications of psycho-linguistics to problems of reading among the deaf. In O. Krohnert (Ed.), *Proceedings, International Congress on the Deaf.* Book in preparation, 1980.

POTTER, R.J., KOPP, G.A., & GREEN, H.G. *Visible Speech.* New York: Van Nostrand, 1948.

POTTER, R.J., KOPP, G.A., & KOPP, H.G. *Visible Speech.* New York: Dover Press, 1966.

Extend the learning process.
The FM PHONIC EAR®

Binaural wireless auditory training system for any learning environment.

The HC 431 **FM PHONIC EAR** is a binaural FM auditory training system. **FM PHONIC EAR** was developed because hearing-impaired students have individual amplification needs for good speech discrimination. Anywhere direct communication is needed, you will find HC 431 **FM PHONIC EAR** the auditory training system of choice.

Student/Teacher Mobility

Student and teacher are both mobile. This allows varied educational experiences both indoors and out. Visual indicators allow instructor to monitor the system's operation while in use.

Speech Reception Unexcelled

Achieved via undistorted, clear amplification, correct frequency response and high signal-to-noise ratio controlled by patented compression.

Speech Discrimination Improvement

Teacher speech level is constant. This is particularly important in the presence of background and room noise.

Adjusts Easily to Acoustic Needs

To best meet personal acoustic needs, each student

unit is adjustable by the educational audiologist. There are seven discrete-position frequency response adjustments possible plus seven discrete-position SSPL controls which individually pre-set the maximum power output. Students have separate controls available for their Most Comfortable Listening level.

Audio Input Capability

Enhances listening conditions with audio-visual materials.

Multiple Service Centers

Regional and international service centers are in strategic locations. Down-time is reduced should service be required.

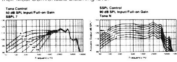

World's leading supplier of hearing, language and speech instruments.

USA:	Canada:	Outside North America:
Phonic Ear Inc.	*Phonic Ear Ltd.*	*Phonic Ear International A/S*
250 Camino Alto	7475 Kimbel Street Unit 10	Formervangen 34
Mill Valley, CA 94941	Mississauga, Ont. L5S 1E7 ·	DK 2600 Glostrup
415/383-4000	Canada	Copenhagen, Denmark
	416/677-3231	Phone (02) 45 85 66

Into the Mainstream of Education

Vira J. Froehlinger, Editor

Today's Hearing Impaired Child provides a comprehensive, "how-to" guide to use when hearing impaired children are being considered for, or placed in mainstream programs.

- *Parents* will benefit from an overall view of their child's educational opportunities and rights.

- *Teachers* will be able to find the answers to most of the questions and concerns felt by teachers facing a special/regular classroom.

- *Administrators* will receive a useful general background on mainstreaming. This book also is an excellent text for in-service training.

Softcover—$14.95 plus .75 handling.
ORDERS MUST BE PREPAID.
To order write:

A.G. Bell Publications
3417 Volta Place, N.W.
Washington, D.C. 20007

1981-82 Fort Lauderdale Seminars

October 28, 1981 — Geoffrey P. Ivimey, Ph.D.
A.G.Bell International Lecturer
The Psychological Bases of the Oral Education of Deaf Children

December 7-11, 1981 — Father Anthony vanUden, Ph.D.
The Conversational and Discovery Approach to the Acquisition of Language and Speech by Deaf Children

April 19-22, 1982 — Susann Schmid-Giovannini
Better and More Enjoyable Reading for Deaf Children Through Listening and Speech

Continuing Education Units Available

For registration information contact:
Fort Lauderdale Oral Education Center
3100 S.W. 8th Avenue
Fort Lauderdale, Florida 33315
Attention: Jack R. Mills, D.Sc.

Double The Effectiveness Of Your Speech Training

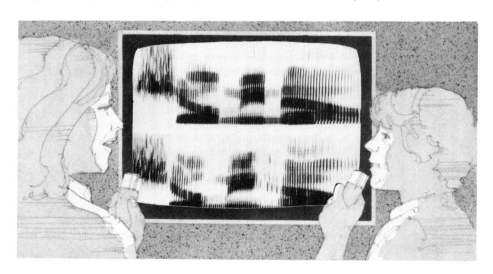